The Enemy of Ignorance

facts, trivia, & general knowledge

Elsmere Gracey

Dedicated to Sandra...

Also available on Amazon and Kindle

The Smarty Pants Series

- Clever Knickers – facts & general knowledge.

- Smarter Than Yesterday – facts, trivia, & general knowledge.

- Smarter Every Day – facts, trivia, & general knowledge

- Smarter Every Year – 366 Random Facts

- Extracts From The Smarty Pants Series – facts, trivia, & general knowledge

*"What we know is a drop, what we don't know is
an ocean."*

Isaac Newton

*"It's an inspiration that one person found knowledge
itself to be the most beautiful thing."*

Bill Gates on Leonardo da Vinci

*"The more you learn, the more you have a framework that
the knowledge fits into."*

Bill Gates

"The world is made up of facts, not things."

Ludwig Wittgenstein

*"The greatest enemy of knowledge is not ignorance, it is
the illusion of knowledge."*

Daniel J. Boorstin

From January 1920 until December 1933, the prohibition in the United States was a nationwide constitutional ban on the production, importation, transportation, and sale of alcohol. It was advocated by activists who were under the impression that removing alcohol from society would be the country's cure for loose morals, domestic abuse, poor health, and anti-social behaviour.

For those that rebelled, the solution was to hide a flask in the top part of a tall boot. This idea had been around for many centuries and had previously been used to conceal knives and guns, and to smuggle goods – even babies. The act of hiding alcohol and other items in the leg of a boot became known as "bootlegging". The term spread into general reference and became generalised for something unlawful – which has endured to this day.

During prohibition, many women bootleggers didn't get caught as they were protected by specific laws which prohibited women from being searched. For those that ended up in court, they discovered that juries were more lenient on women, in particular, those that were mothers and grandmothers. One famous bootlegger was Maggie Bailey who became a legend in Harbin County, Kentucky, and earned herself the title of "Queen of the Mountain Bootleggers". Bailey started to sell moonshine when she was just 17-years-old. She was convicted once and served eighteen months in prison but, once released, went straight back into the business until she retired at the age of 95. Bailey never drank herself and refused to serve children or adults who had an alcohol problem. She was loved by everyone in the community for both her warm, grandmotherly appearance and the fact that she sold her moonshine on credit and allowed others to sell it on to make some money themselves.

Before she passed away in 2005, at the age of 101, she claimed that the excitement of her job kept her young.

*

Aeroplane manufacturers design and build planes that have standard row positioning, i.e. each row of seats are aligned to a window. However, to make the seating arrangements as flexible as possible, there are multiple tracks on the floors, and ultimately, it is the decision of the airline where the seats will be positioned.

Airlines make their profit by filling as many seats as possible. To maximise ticket sales, the seating is adjusted to fit as many as possible on the plane. This explains why many rows do not align with the windows.

*

Baobabs are found in Madagascar, Africa, and Australia, and are easily recognised by their thick trunks and swollen stems. These trunks can reach between 23 to 36 feet in diameter and 16 to 98 feet in height. One tree that collapsed in Namibia during 2015 was thought to be around 1,275 years old although carbon dating indicates that they may actually live for up to 3,000 years.

Nicknamed as the *upside-down-tree* due to the root-like appearance of their tangled branches, baobabs are also known as the *tree of life* as they create their own ecosystem which supports the existence of large mammals, and thousands of small creatures that live in its crevices.

Bushmen don't believe that the trees actually grow, but instead, they crash to earth in a fully-formed state. Another belief about the tree is that it will help a young boy grow to be tall and strong if he is washed in water that has been soaked in the tree's bark.

The western world has recently viewed the fruit of the baobab as the ultimate super-fruit; this is due to its high quantities of vitamin C, calcium, iron, and potassium. It is not only recommended for weight loss and skin elasticity, but also for improving cardiovascular health.

*

The sclerocarya birrea - a tree commonly known as the marula, is found in Africa and Madagascar. The trees have a specific gender, which leads to the belief that bark infusions can be used to influence the gender of an unborn child. Depending on what the parents want, they will use either the male or female tree to make the infusions. However, should a baby of the opposite sex be born, it is deemed to be special as it was able to defy the spirits.

The marula bears fruits from January to March. After a few weeks, the marula fruit becomes overripe and drops from the tree supplying a bountiful feast for all the animals. However, as it quickly ferments in their stomachs the animals begin to stumble about and fall over – a similar scene as Belfast on a Friday night!

*

Mirror-writing is very common amongst children when they are learning to write. Traditionally it was thought that this reflected slow intellectual development, but this myth has since been dismissed. Instead, it is now accepted that children do this as they tend to face each character in the same direction as the preceding one. Researchers also concluded that the action implies that the general shape of a character is learned before the direction it should be written in.

The most common usage of mirror writing is found on the front of an ambulance; this is so drivers can view the word the correct way around when they look in their rear-view mirror.

Leonardo da Vinci used a variation of mirrored writing - he started at the right side of the page and wrote to the left. The only time that he wrote in the normal direction was when it was intended for other people to read.

da Vinci wrote his famous "Codex Leicester" in mirror-writing. The writings detailed his observations and theories on topics such as why fossils can be found on mountains and the luminosity of the moon. However, the central theme was his study of water and innovative ideas for land reclamation, projects for docks, and machines that would make the use of energy supplied by water. The codex was purchased from the Leicester estate in 1980 and after a painstaking process of compiling it back into its original form was sold to Bill Gates in 1994 for a reported $30.8 million which made it the most expensive manuscript in the world. As an avid reader, Gates wanted to share the knowledge contained within the "Codex Leicester" so subsequently made it available to view in selected museums before a digital version became readily accessible.

*

In November 2016, the most expensive piece of clothing purchased at an auction came with a price-tag of $4.8 million. It was the jewel-encrusted dress that Marilyn Monroe wore when she serenaded "Happy Birthday" to President J. F. Kennedy in 1962. It was purchased by "Ripley's Believe it or Not!".

It had been previously purchased for $1,267,500 in 1999 by Robert Schargen - the clothing president for the Manhattan-based collectable company "Gotta Have it".

The dress originally cost $12,000.

*

A group of chicks is called a chattering.

*

When rain falls on dry ground, an earthy scent called *petrichor* is produced.

*

The Barbican in London is a world-renowned multi-arts and conference venue which attracts over 1.1 million visitors annually. It is home to the "Rain Room" which is a 100-metre^2 area of pouring rain which people can walk through without getting wet. 3D cameras turn individual valves on and off as they sense someone walking about.

*

An elephant calf often sucks its trunk for comfort in the same way that a human baby sucks its thumb.

Although it is more common in the early stages of life, it is not uncommon for older elephants to do it, even old bulls, especially when they are feeling nervous.

*

In Japan, some retailers have *bohan yu kara boru* positioned next to the cash registers. These items are plastic spheres filled with brightly coloured liquid pigment which are supposed to be thrown at robbers during a heist with the intent of permanently staining their clothes to improve the likelihood of authorities identifying and catching them.

Although their usage has proven limited, they have been responsible for the crime rate decreasing as they act as a deterrent. They were created some thirty years ago as a replacement for raw eggs which were thrown at cars that drove through tolls without paying.

*

On the 6th August 1945, Tsutomu Yamaguchi (1916-2010) was on his last day of a business trip in Hiroshima when the atomic bomb fell. He suffered burns to his face and forearms and both his eardrums were ruptured. The following day, Yamaguchi managed to get a train bound for his hometown of Nagasaki. His blackened burns and injuries made him unrecognisable to his family and friends, yet despite being on the verge of collapse, he arrived to work on the morning of 9th August. A few hours later an atomic bomb landed two miles away which shattered the office windows blowing his bandages off and exposing him to another surge of cancer-causing radiation.

Over the next few days Yamaguchi's hair fell out, his wounds turned gangrenous, and he vomited uncontrollably. However, unlike many other victims exposed to the bomb, Yamaguchi recovered and lived a relatively normal life until he passed away at the age of 93. It is estimated that around 165 people may have survived both bombs, but Yamaguchi is the only person officially recognised by the Japanese government for doing so.

*

Scientists had reason to suspect that crows were able to recognise human faces. To prove their theory, they decided to wear masks to capture crows to band them. After being released, they found that in every case the crows recognised and scolded whenever someone approached wearing the same mask that had been worn when they were captured. However, when someone approached in a different mask, there was no reaction. It was recorded that the birds would hold a grudge for over three years.

*

During the early 1960s, excavations took place in Israel at the site of Herod the Great's palace. A small jar, dating back some 2,000 years, was discovered which contained seeds. After being stored until 2005, a botanical researcher decided to plant one to see if anything would grow – the result was the growth of a Judean date palm tree. Not only has the seed become the oldest tree seed to germinate, but it also breathed life back into a tree that had been driven into extinction.

*

One of Iran's thirty-one provinces is West Azerbaijan in which lies the rural village of Kahrar-e Dejgah. The 2006 census recorded the population as just 94 of which one resident was Amou Haji who has become known as the world's dirtiest man. Haji hasn't washed for over sixty years, and with the dirt deeply ingrained he has almost become the same colour as the earth, and so blends in with his surroundings.

Haji resides in a hole in the ground which he believes keeps him in touch with reality (although he does have the option to take shelter in an open brick shack that the villagers constructed for him).

His favourite meal is rotten porcupine meat. Each day he drinks five litres of water which is stored in a large rusty oil can. He smokes five cigarettes at a time, but should he decide to smoke his pipe, he fills it with animal faeces instead of tobacco.

Haji is open to the idea of a relationship but only on the condition that the woman of his dreams accepts his alternative lifestyle.

*

The earliest version of a treadmill was introduced in the late part of the first century (A.D.). The idea surfaced again during the 1800s when they were made suitable for animals which enabled their owners to use them for domestic purposes such as powering machinery for butter churns, grinding stones, and fanning mills.

A tread-wheel was introduced to prisons in 1818 to help reform stubborn and idle convicts. During a gruelling eight-hour shift, prisoners would climb the equivalent of 7,200 feet on a large paddle wheel which would crush grain or pump water (although sometimes the labour served no purpose other than punishment). It was eventually abandoned for being too cruel under the Prisons Act, and the treadmill was almost lost to history for a second time. It reappeared in 1952 when a cardiologist, Dr Robert Bruce, used a modernised version in a bid to monitor and diagnose various heart conditions.

Throughout the 1960s and 1970s, treadmills were marketed for home/gym exercise. They are recognised as reducing joint stress by up to 30% when compared to running on footpaths.

On the 20th August 2016, Ronnie Delzer (USA) achieved the world record for running the furthermost distance of 89.38 miles (143.84 km) on a treadmill in twelve hours. This beat the record set just two months earlier by Dave Proctor of Calgary who had completed 86.49 miles (139.2 km) which had exceeded the previous record set in February 2016.

*

According to the WWF, there are 1,864 wild pandas in the world which are mostly found in the Sichuan province of South-West China. Previously classified as an endangered species, the slow but steady increase in population has resulted in them being removed from the endangered list and classified as vulnerable.

However, some sub-species, such as the brown-white panda, are extremely rare. Since 1985, there have only been five sightings; the only confirmed living brown-white panda is known as Qi Zia (believed to have been born in 2000). Scientists theorise that the colouring could either have links with the unique geographical and climate conditions or that it could be the result of a double recessive gene.

Qi Zia was found as a two-month-old cub who had been abandoned by his mother. When Qi Zia began living at the nature reserve, he was bullied by other pandas who also ate his bamboo. Despite all odds, he survived and has grown to weigh more than 200 lbs (which is considered the average size for a panda of his age). He can eat up to 110 lbs of bamboo every day, which helps him survive the cold weather – that is roughly the same as a person eating 25 chickens each day.

Pandas are renowned for being lazy – their busy schedule consists of foraging for food and having long rests. They are mostly carnivores but move too slowly to catch live prey.

Breeding is not high on their list of priorities, which is one of the reasons that they became endangered; there is only one day in the year that females can conceive naturally. Another reason that they became endangered is that they defecate in the direction they are travelling, which made it easy for them to be tracked by those who believed their pelt provided magical protection against evil spirits. Loss of habitat also added to their decline in number.

On average, a new-born panda weighs just 100 grams (0.2 lbs) which is 1/900th of their mother's weight. It measures 15 cms long.

Pandas have seven digits on their paws. The sixth acts as a thumb; the seventh is called the pisiform, which helps it to grasp bamboo.

A panda's gut is covered with a thick layer of mucus which protects it against bamboo splinters.

*

During the winter months, Alaskan Wood Frogs (which have a life span of four to six years) survive by freezing; two-thirds of their body fluid turns to ice, their heart stops beating, their blood stops flowing, and their glucose levels spiral.

In preparation for this event, the frogs spend a few weeks freezing during the night and thawing out the next day. When the temperature drops permanently below freezing, they go into a deep freeze during which time they are not able to communicate nor move. If the frog was picked up and had its legs straightened during this period the legs would actually break.

They have been known to withstand temperatures as low as -16°C before thawing and returning to their normal healthy state.

When spring arrives seven months later, they thaw and happily hop away.

*

The word "bully" was reportedly first used in 1530 A.D. and applied to both genders – it meant *sweetheart*. It appears to have Dutch and German roots from words that mean *lover* or *brother*.

In the 1600s, the meaning began to change. During this period it started to be used to describe someone brave, then to mean *a protector of prostitutes*, until in the 1780s it referred to a coward who becomes a terror to the weak.

Social bullying is often harder to recognise and can be carried out behind backs without the victim's knowledge. The bully will spread lies about their victim, encourage others to socially exclude them, damage their reputation, or play jokes to intentionally embarrass and humiliate them.

In 2014, a judge in Ohio ordered Edmond Aviv, a 62-year-old bully, to stand on a street corner wearing a sign declaring that he was a bully because he had harassed his neighbours and their disabled child for 15 years. Aviv was also sentenced to fifteen days' imprisonment.

*

Tanzanite is the trade name for the blue coloured mineral zoisite. It was discovered in Northern Tanzania in 1967, which is the only place in the world that it has been found. It is a very rare gemstone mined in an area of just 4 kms^2 and is hailed as the most beautiful gemstone to be discovered in 2,000 years.

In 2002, Tanzanite became the first gemstone since 1912 to be added to the birthstone list by the American Gem Trade Association – it shares December with zircon and turquoise.

The average price of Tanzanite is $1,000 per carat.

*

The most expensive gemstone is the red diamond, which has a price tag of around $1 million per carat. There are less than thirty red diamonds in the world, most of which are less than one carat. The largest weighed an impressive 13.90 carats in its rough state when it was found by a farmer in Brazil during the mid-1990s. It lost 8.79 carats during the cut, but the transformation was amazing. Initially known as the "Red Shield" it was renamed "The Moussaieff Red Diamond" when it was purchased in the early 2000s for $8 million. The buyer, Shlomo Moussaieff (1925-2015), was an Israeli-born jewellery dealer in London; it is presently owned by Moussaieff Jewellers Ltd.

*

The residents of Great Britain eat more tins of baked beans than the rest of the world combined – one tin of Heinz baked beans is sold every seventeen seconds.

There are approximately 465 beans in a 415-grams can.

British Labour MP, Viscount Simon (Jan David Simon), allegedly asked during a session in the House of Lords whether there could be a link between global warming and the smelly emissions that are released when taking into consideration the large number of baked beans consumed within the U.K.!

*

During the 1970s, the average dairy cow produced around 825 gallons (3,750 litres) of milk each year. Due to the introduction of selective breeding, and the intensification of herd management, the output gradually increased - by 2012 the average production was 2,500 gallons (11,365 litres) a year.

In January 2017, it was reported that a cow in Wisconsin, called *My Gold*, produced more than 9,000 gallons of milk in one year. The record had previously been held by My Gold's mother, who had produced approximately 8,000 gallons in one year.

Researchers in Poland observed that children raised on lactose-free formulas or milk-free diets had problems with developing proper bone mass as the subjects had lower levels of the chemical markers required for bone formation as well as higher vitamin D deficiencies.

Another Polish study observed that children who were supplied with raw milk had a lower occurrence of asthma, allergies, hay fever, and chronic nasal congestion. Their results supported the hypothesis that raw milk protects against allergies and other autoimmune-related diseases. Science has demonstrated that raw milk contains nutrients destroyed by pasteurisation.

*

According to legend, the Milky Way was accidentally created when drops of breast milk leaked from Hera, the wife of Zeus, as she breast-fed Hercules.

*

Not only does buffalo milk contain 25% more protein than cow's milk but it is claimed that it is more of a health benefit as it helps to: - reduce eczema, reduce the symptoms of irritable bowel syndrome, build strong bones, promote growth, protect the heart, stimulate circulation, and lower blood pressure. One of the explanations for this is that buffalos seem to have a stronger immune system. Also, they have not been given as many antibiotics as dairy cows.

True buffalo (as opposed to American bison) only live in Africa and Asia.

*

The Peace Bridge, which connects Buffalo, America, with Fort Erie, Canada, was officially opened in 1927.

It is the second busiest U.S.A./Canada border crossing; the busiest is the Ambassador Bridge between Detroit and the city of Windsor in Ontario.

*

The French manufactures of beetroot alcohol asked Louis Pasteur to investigate the reason their product was turning sour. Upon analysing random samples taken from the vats, he discovered thousands of micro-organisms which he believed were responsible for the problem. His research led him to work on other liquids such as milk, wine, and vinegar. He concluded that they were all being contaminated with microbes that float in the air. Although his research was questioned, with many people telling him that he was wrong, he continued with the project and eventually proved his theory correct. Against peer pressure, he went on to create the process of pasteurisation.

*

When someone coughs, air shoots out of their lungs in a jet several feet long. Thousands of tiny droplets of saliva are also forced out at up to 50 miles per hour. If someone coughs without covering their mouth, the germs can travel about 3 metres.

The body naturally produces between 1 to 1.5 litres of phlegm every day, but when mucus is coughed up, it usually indicates that the person has an allergy or an infection. It occurs as a result of the respiratory tract becoming inflamed, which also leads to coughing.

- Clear phlegm is considered normal.

- White/grey phlegm may indicate an upper respiratory tract infection or sinus congestion.

- If it is thick and coloured green/dark yellow, it suggests that a viral or bacterial infection is present. The body's immune system responds by sending white blood cells to the infected area. These cells contain a green protein which changes the colour of the mucus.

- The most likely reason for phlegm to be brown is that the person is a smoker. However, it could be due to their diet if it contains chocolate, coffee, and red wine. Smokers phlegm can have a grainy texture.

- Pink phlegm may indicate that there is fluid in the lungs (Pulmonary oedema).

- Blood in phlegm may be a sign of bronchitis.

Some reports claim that swallowing phlegm is harmful, while others argue that there is no risk to the person's health because stomach acids and enzymes will neutralise the microbes.

*

People who are impervious to pain can also be insensitive to touch. Scientists believe that this is because both senses share a common pathway in the spinal cord known as the spinothalamic tract. This explains why there are many similarities between pain and an itch, such as: -

- both can be triggered by chemicals, heat, and force,

- both can sometimes be relieved by anti-inflammatory drugs,

- both are related to anxiety and attention.

However, some medications may suppress pain, but in turn, make an itch worse. Scratching may relieve an itch, but it may induce pain.

One thing that scientists still don't understand is how the inside of a person's mouth can get itchy, but their stomach doesn't, yet a stomach can get painful but not itchy!

A study in 2014 found that the naturally occurring chemical, serotonin, is the connection between an itch and a pain. In the brain, serotonin plays a role in mood, circadian rhythms, and hallucinations, whereas in the stomach, serotonin helps to control the ill effects of food which cause diarrhoea. In the skin, serotonin plays the role of either inhibiting pain or exacerbating an itch.

The scientific name for itching is *pruritus,* which is caused by the gene known as *gastrin-releasing peptide receptor*. One theory to explain why people scratch is that the action prevents specific neurons found in the spinal column from sending signals to the brain. However, scratching a painful itch, such as a mosquito bite, will make it itch more. This happens because scratching causes pain which the body controls by immediately producing serotonin, which in turn makes the area itchier.

A study, led by a cognitive neuroscientist, was conducted at "Liverpool John Moores University" whereby participants were shown a range of images that were either itch-inducing or neutral and then asked how itchy they felt. It was found that visual cues could provoke the itch sensation in people, but they were most reactive when watching another person scratching rather than seeing the cause of the itch. Another study, which included brain scans, showed that the same parts of the brain are activated when watching someone else scratch as when someone does it to themselves - mirror neurons activate when someone observes the behaviour.

*

The famous American actress, activist, and author, Shirley MacLaine, is the sister of Warren Beatty, the famous American actor and filmmaker.

*

The original Old Testament writings were in Hebrew while the New Testament was in Greek. In 382 A.D. Pope Damasus I commissioned St. Jerome to translate the Bible into Latin. This translation became known as the Vulgate and has become the official Roman Catholic Bible.

The first hand-written English manuscripts were produced in the 1380s by John Wycliffe who translated from the Latin Vulgate. Forty-four years after Wycliffe's death, the Pope ordered his bones to be dug up, crushed, and scattered in a river as he was so outraged by Wycliffe's teaching and translation into English.

*

Sandra Clarke, while working as a nurse at the "Sacred Heart Medical Centre" in Oregon, was asked by a frail elderly gentleman on his deathbed if she would stay with him. She told him that she would return after she finished her ward-round. Unfortunately, by the time Clarke returned to visit him, he had passed away. Although overcome with guilt that the patient had died alone, she channelled the emotions into an idea to create a program known as "No One Dies Alone".

Since the program started in 2001, it has spread throughout America as well as being introduced to Singapore and Japan.

There are many reasons why people die alone. Volunteers have held the hands of those known as "elder orphans" (older people who have outlived their families), those who have been travelling or lived a long distance away from any family members, people who do not want to die in front of their loved ones, and those who have been alienated by their family and friends.

*

The first wiki, a website developed by a community of users which allows any user to edit the content, was designed by Howard G "Ward" Cunningham, an American computer programmer.

In the online world, Cunningham realised that the best way to get a conversation started in a community chatroom was to make an incorrect statement rather than by asking a question; human nature is that people prefer to correct others when the opportunity arises rather than to answer a question. This has become known as "Cunningham's Law".

*

Keiko (whose name means "Lucky One" in Japanese) was a

male orca who became famous after starring in the 1993 movie "Free Willy".

In 1979, Keiko was captured in Iceland and for the next three years lived in an Icelandic aquarium in Hafnarfjörður. He was then sold to Marineland in Ontario where he was forced to perform for public entertainment. His ownership subsequently passed to an amusement park in Mexico City where conditions were deplorable, and animals were poorly treated – any animals unwilling to work were deprived of food as a punishment. The water Keiko swam in was warm tap-water mixed with sacks of salt; as a result of the unsuitable environment, he suffered rashes due to viral infections and had ongoing stomach upsets for which regular medication was required. Frustrated, he began to self-harm by having prolonged sessions of pushing his head against the pool wall. However, regardless of the inhospitable living conditions, he remained kind, gentle, and patient.

Following his appearance in three movies, Warner Bros. Studio decided to find him a more suitable home. The "Free-Willy-Keiko Foundation" was established in 1995 and approximately $7 million was raised, which enabled the building of appropriate facilities to nurse Keiko back to good health before returning him to the wild. This led to a lot of controversy with some arguing that he would not survive in the wild after spending so long in captivity. The suggestion was even made to have him killed and the meat sent to Africa as foreign aid.

Keiko's first step back to freedom began by living in a specially built rehabilitation centre on the Oregon coast before moving on to a purpose-built sea pen floating inside a small cove in Iceland (although the flight to Iceland was rather eventful as the aircraft suffered a landing gear failure).

Following several months in the sea pen, Keiko was allowed to swim around the cove. After a VHF tracking device was fixed to his body, he was eventually allowed out to the ocean where he was accompanied on short journeys by a boat. This became routine for approximately two years until the day came that he didn't return to his restricted freedom; sometime later Keiko's VHF signal indicated that he was some seven hundred miles away in Norway making him the first captive orca to be successfully returned to the wild.

Although he left Norway with a pod of orcas in August 2000 he showed up sometime later in Norway's Skålvik Fjord seeking contact with humans – he even allowed children to ride on his back. Those that had been opposed to returning Keiko to the wild used this action to argue that his release had not been successful as he did not know how to integrate properly with unrelated orcas and considered humans as companions.

Keiko passed away in December 2003. It was estimated that he was approximately 26-years-old. The suspected cause of Keiko's death was pneumonia.

Under normal circumstances, Norwegian fisheries management would have ordered the remains of a large sea mammal to be towed to sea and sunk into deep water. However, Keiko was buried in a snow-bound pasture in a secret ceremony with only seven mourners in attendance. Once the grave location was made known to the public, school children from the village placed stones on top of the grave to create the traditional burial mound; visitors continually add to the ever-growing pile. Some people suspect that Keiko was buried on land so that in time his skeleton can be dug up and placed in a museum.

*

Orcas are the largest members of the dolphin family.

On average, a wild male orca's life-span is around twenty-nine years, although the maximum is recorded as sixty.

Like wolves, orcas hunt in packs and are known as the *wolves of the sea* due to their talented hunting skills.

*

The author of Sherlock Holmes was Arthur Ignatius Conan Doyle (1859 to 1930), a Scotsman born in Edinburgh.

During his studies to become a doctor, Doyle was offered the opportunity to be a ship's surgeon on a whaling boat headed for the Arctic Circle. With a deep-rooted love for writing, this real-life adventure found its way into his first story which was about the sea and entitled "Captain of the Pole-Star".

Torn between the idea of having a medical career or being an author, he decided to open an ophthalmology practice. Although he never had one single client come through his door, he was undeterred as this gave him time to put thoughts onto paper and he completed writing a series of short stories.

The character of Sherlock Holmes was based on one of Doyle's teachers, Dr Joseph Bell, who was a master at observation, logic, deduction, and diagnosis.

In time, Doyle felt that the character of Sherlock Holmes oppressed him, so he decided to have Holmes plunged to his death at the Reichenbach Falls in Switzerland. In memory of Holmes, the "Sherlock Holmes Museum" is based at the address where the fictional character lived – 221b Baker Street, London. The building, which is officially between 237 and 241 Baker Street, is protected by the government due to its architectural and historical interest.

Doyle had aspirations for other career opportunities as well. He volunteered as a soldier during the Boer War but was turned down because of his weight. Not discouraged by this rejection, he volunteered as a doctor for which he was accepted. He also ran for an assembly seat in Central Edinburgh but was accused of being a Catholic bigot. His interests then turned to the occult, and he went on psychic crusades to America, Australia, and Africa, the events of which were reflected in his writings.

Following a heart-attack, Doyle died surrounded by his family. His last words were to his (second) wife to whom he said: "you are wonderful".

*

Pistanthrophobia is the fear of trusting people based on previous relationship experiences.

*

Terpenes are a class of organic hydrocarbons which are produced by a large variety of plants. Often they emit a strong odour which protects them from predators.

The alpha-pinene terpene is one of the most powerful; it is responsible for giving evergreen trees the fresh earthy scent. Studies have shown that alpha-pinenes offer many health benefits, which include anti-cancer properties, anti-inflammatory benefits, antibiotic properties, as well as increasing alertness and counteracting anxiety. This explains why people can feel refreshed after walking through a pine forest.

*

When Ruth Coker Burks was a young girl, her mother and her uncle had a massive row - as a result, Ruth's mother purchased 262 plots in the local cemetery to ensure family members would not be buried beside each other.

In 1984, when Burks was 25-years-old, she was visiting a friend in hospital when she noticed the door of a side-ward was covered with a red bag. She watched as nurses drew straws as to who would go in to check on the patient. Burks guessed that the patient was suffering from a new epidemic knows as GRID (gay-related immune deficiency). Ignoring the warning signs, she sneaked in to see the patient and stayed with him until he passed away some thirteen hours later.

Burks quickly learned that most GRID patients had been disowned by their families and friends and were facing death alone. Word spread that she wasn't afraid of the disease, and she was asked to help others. She would take them to medical appointments, help them to get their medication, and lift their spirits when they felt depressed.

As AIDS was unheard of until that time, there was not the knowledge on how it was transmitted nor procedures in place about delivering medical care, which resulted in immense fear. When Burks would collect prescriptions at the chemist, they would make her keep the pen that she had touched in case it was carrying any of the germs. They would follow her to the door while spraying disinfectant behind her.

Berks helped many patients to fill out their own death certificate as she knew that once they were gone, she wouldn't be able to get the information from family members.

Over ten years, Burks estimated that she helped to care for more than one thousand people dying of AIDS. Many were buried in the plots that her mother had purchased; Burks even dug forty-three graves herself, sometimes assisted by her young daughter.

Burks was a childhood friend of Bill Clinton's. When he was elected president, Burks served as a White House consultant on AIDS education.

*

An ancient Japanese technique can help relieve emotions within a short time frame. The belief is that each digit on our hands represents a different kind of emotion and by simply massaging each digit the feeling fades: -

- The thumb helps to fend off emotions such as anxiety and worry,
- The index finger represents fear,
- The middle finger helps to control anger,
- The ring finger is for sadness, and
- The small finger is to relieve stress. It also boosts optimism and self-esteem.

*

Inner speech (the voice you hear when you think or read) is accompanied by tiny muscular movements in the larynx. The left inferior frontal gyrus (Broca area) is also fired up just like it is when speaking out loud.

*

William Harvey (1578-1657) was an English physician who was the first person to accurately describe how the heart pumped blood around the body. He made observations by cutting living animals open and viewing how the blood flowed through veins and arteries.

Although his research methods were cruel, it was an advancement on the knowledge that Galen had taught. Galen's findings resulted in him having to flee from Rome as his knowledge and methods threatened the careers of quack physicians; likewise, Harvey's career also took a dive following a bombardment of criticism that he received from other physicians.

Harvey was also the first to propose that reproduction occurred when an egg was fertilised by sperm.

*

Giordano Bruno (1548 to 1600) was an Italian Dominican friar, philosopher, mathematician, poet, and cosmological theorist who believed that the sun, not the earth, was the centre of the solar system and proposed that there was an infinite cosmos which consisted of countless heliocentric worlds. He also developed a theory whereby everything that existed was made of identical particles and that God resided in these elements.

In 1593, Bruno was tried by the Roman Inquisition for heresy, and his writings were listed on the Church's "Index of Forbidden Books". On the 16th February 1600, he was taken from his cell in the early hours of the morning to be burnt alive at a stake. Executioners were ordered to tie his tongue to ensure he was unable to address the crowd.

Today, Bruno is considered as a free-thinker and a martyr of science. A crater on the far side of the moon is named in his honour.

*

In the spring of 1952, John W. Hetrick, his wife, and their daughter were in a car accident. The first reaction of both adults was to put their arms out to stop their daughter from hitting the dashboard. The incident prompted the retired engineering technician to design an object that would be activated during an accident to prevent passengers from striking the interior of the car. In 1953, he obtained a patent for a safety cushion.

In the same year, a German inventor called William Linderer also received a patent for an inflatable cushion that protected drivers in the event of an accident.

These designs inspired the motor industry to develop safety features: -

- In 1967, Mercedes-Benz started to develop airbags as we know them today.

- In 1973, the Oldsmobile Toronado became the first car with a passenger airbag.

- The Porsche 944 Turbo was the first car to have both driver and passenger airbags as standard equipment.

- In 1990, Ford was the first manufacturer to make airbags standard equipment in their vehicles.

*

During migration from Europe to Africa and Asia, approximately five-hundred-million birds from more than five hundred species, pass through Israel every year. The phenomena, which was recorded in Biblical times when mentioned by Jeremiah, attracts thousands of bird-watchers every year.

*

Back in the 1920s, the newlywed Earle Dickson would come home from his job as a cotton buyer at the American company "Johnson and Johnson" to find his dinner on the table courtesy of this wife, Josephine. Diligent with household duties but slightly accident-prone, Josephine would often suffer minor cuts and burns on her fingers. Together they would cut pieces of adhesive tape and cotton gauze to make bandages.

To be prepared for such events, Dickson created some ready-made bandages by placing squares of cotton gauze at intervals along adhesive strips and covered them with crinoline. An informal discussion with his boss about the invention led to the first adhesive bandages being produced and sold under the Band-Aid® tradename. Dickson was promoted to the position of Vice President.

*

Whitter is a small remote town in Alaska which is often referred to as *the town under one roof*.

Almost all of the town's 217 residents live in the same building called "Begich Towers" which was purpose-built in 1974 as an army barracks. Besides being home to so many, it also contains a police station, a church, a clinic, a grocery store, and offers bed & breakfast facilities. Children don't even have to leave the building to go to school as an underground passage leads directly to the Whittier Community School.

It is a slight misconception that everyone lives under the same roof as there are, in fact, a small number of apartments separate from the main building, where approximately 20% of the residents live.

Whitter is subjected to six months of snow every year

accompanied by howling winds of up to 80 miles per hour.

Depending on the weather, the town can be reached by either boat or by an underground tunnel (which was originally a railway line). However, if choosing the tunnel as a means of travel be prepared for a half-hour wait at the traffic lights as the direction of the single-lane traffic only changes every thirty minutes.

*

On the 11th February 2017, Belfast, Northern Ireland, held its first-ever "Ginger Pride Festival". The aim was to celebrate all things ginger and began with a street party which included live music by ginger musicians along with other activities such as gingerbread decorating. With five-hundred ginger-haired people attending it became the largest gathering on record of gingers together in one place in Ireland.

*

An Australian tabloid, the Courier-Mail, published an article in 2007 which claimed that genetic scientists believed redheads were becoming rare and could actually be extinct within the next one-hundred years. Some experts thought it could happen sooner than that and red-heads would be gone by 2060.

The argument for their claim was that global intermingling would supply more options with blonde and brown heads being more desirable. This would result in the gene MC1R (melanocortin 1 receptor - which is the recessive gene responsible for red hair) slipping into obscurity.

Another argument was made in 2014 by Dr Alistair Moffat from the University of St Andrews, Scotland, who hypothesised that the change in the planet's climate would see the gene being less required.

However, geneticists around the world have refuted both claims as genes can be dormant for a few generations before reappearing.

*

Rikers Island is New York's main prison complex as well as the name of the 413-acre island on which it sits. The only way to get onto the island is via a bridge which inmates have nicknamed as *the bridge of pain*.

The island is named after a Dutch settler, Abraham Rycken, who moved to Long Island in 1638; his descendants owned the island until 1884.

There are usually 12,000 male and female inmates – mostly pre-trial defendants who cannot afford to pay bail, and nonviolent offenders serving short sentences.

The prison is notorious for being a culture of abuse. Inmates are sent to solidarity confinement for minor infractions and can be kept there for months at a time. These cells have solid concrete walls with a window so small it hardly can be seen through. Prisoners are allowed outside for one hour each day, but even then, it is only into a separate outdoor cage.

One document claimed that 57% of inmates in solidarity confinement were initially serving sentences for non-violent crimes but were being punished for outbursts of anger.

Besides having America's highest rate of solitary confinement, Rikers Island is also known for inmate violence, staff brutality, rape, and abuse of adolescents and those with mental health issues. One investigation uncovered a secret society run by correctional officers that encouraged prisoners to extort and beat other inmates in the name of maintaining order; this was known as the *program*.

On the 1st February 1957, a plane crash-landed on Rikers Island minutes after taking off from La Guardia airport on a flight to Miami. Twenty of the 91 passengers were killed as a result of the crash and explosion. Fifty-seven inmates took part in the rescue mission of the crash survivors and afterwards were rewarded by either being released or having their sentence reduced.

*

The remote Galápagos Islands are home to the Blue-Footed Booby. In the 1960s the islands were home to almost 50% of the world's breeding pairs. Their name originates from the Spanish word *bobo* meaning *foolish* or *clown* which was probably given to them because of the clumsy way they walk and possibly because they do not fear humans.

Their blue webbed feet are the most distinctive feature and play an important role in courtship - the bluer the feet are, the more attractive the bird will appear to a partner. The male whistles loudly to get the attention of the females and then struts around, showing off his feet.

After mating, both parents look after the nest and keep the eggs incubated by placing them on top of their feet. The Blue-Footed Booby is one of the few species of birds that will do its best to care for all of the young and not just those that are most likely to survive.

By 2012 the estimated population had declined to approximately 6,400. It is thought that the decrease in number was as a result of a shortage of clupeid fish, in particular sardines, which the boobies seem to need in large quantities in order to breed.

While their blue feet attract attention from potential mates, they also draw attention from others - yielding to temptation, they often get involved in an extra-marital affair. However, even when caught red-handed, their forgiving partner doesn't react, and the couple renews their vows by a courting ritual and get back to looking after their young.

*

Victor Morrow (1929 – 1982) was an American actor who starred alongside Elvis Presley in the film "King Creole", and appeared in various television shows.

During the filming of the "Twilight Zone: The Movie" he was performing a scene along with two children in which they were trying to escape from an army helicopter. The helicopter was hovering just twenty-four feet above them when it ran into difficulties and crashed. All three actors were killed instantly: Morrow, and 7-year-old Myca Dinh Le were decapitated while 6-year-old Renee Shin-Yi Chen was crushed.

It was a science fiction fantasy horror film produced by Stephen Spielberg and John Landis.

*

It took many years for Christmas tree lights to evolve into what they are today. During the 17th century, wealthy Germans used candles which were strategically placed to illuminate the ornaments that hung from the branches, but they would only be lit for a few minutes at a time while the family sat vigilantly watching with water close by in-case a fire started.

Candle holders came into use around 1900; by 1915 small lanterns and glass balls became a means of holding the candles in place.

Thomas Edison's assistant, Edward Jones, displayed the first set of Christmas tree lights at his home in Manhattan in 1882.

Electric Christmas tree lights got national attention when the 24th President of the USA, Grover Cleveland (1837 to 1908), allowed them to make their debut at the White House in 1895.

By 1908, insurance companies were refusing to pay for damages caused by Christmas tree fires as they deemed burning candles on a dry tree as unsafe!

The basic foundation of the light, i.e. the incandescent bulb barely changed for nearly a century. It was only in recent years that advancement occurred. The popularity of LED lights has increased because of their energy efficiency and the fact that they give off less heat.

One of YouTube's earliest viral videos was in 2005 when Carson Williams, an electrical engineer from Ohio, decorated his house with 25,000 lights which were synchronised to the Trans-Siberian Orchestra's "Wizards in Winter". However, he had to turn the display off as it created an immense traffic jam which resulted in police not being able to attend the scene of a car accident.

*

Mark Sinclair, who is better known by his stage name Vin Diesel, is probably most famous for playing the character of Dominic Toretto in *The Fast and the Furious* movies. When he was 7-years-old, Diesel and his friends broke into a theatre in New York with plans to vandalise it. When they were caught in flagrante delicto, the theatre staff decided not to call the police if the culprits showed up every day for rehearsals. This became his first acting role.

*

While hibernation occurs during the winter, aestivation takes place during the hot, dry summer months. Reptiles, amphibians, and molluscs are the most likely to go through this period of inactivity and lowered metabolic rate. Many disappear underground to stay cooler while in the dormant state.

*

Water contains dissolved minerals such as calcium, iron, magnesium, and sodium. The presence of these minerals is what makes it possible for water to conduct electricity. Water molecules on their own do not have a charge, so consequently, are unable to swap electrons which in turn means that power would be unable to travel.

When water is boiled, and the steam is allowed to condense in a reservoir, it leaves a liquid called distilled water. This liquid is pure as all other chemicals have been removed and therefore electricity would not be able to travel through it.

News circulated when surveillance-camera footage was retrieved following a near-fatal accident in Florida during 2014. Three children were shocked by electricity flowing through a swimming pool which rendered their muscles inactive. Two male adults close by realised something was wrong and risked their own lives to pull the kids to safety. The cause of the accident was traced to a pool pump which had not been earthed correctly and as a result malfunctioned electrifying the water. After four nights in a hospital, the children recovered well enough to go home.

*

There was a claim that before Google introduced g-mail in 2004, the service was actually provided by Garfield.com. It was a company called U.S. Email that owned the gmail.com domain name until they closed down. The domain name passed to a law firm before being obtained by Google.

Garfield.com did offer a similar domain name, which was gmail.garfield.com. The email addresses came with some *cattitude* such as ihatemondays.net; livefurweekends.net; and borntosleep.net.

*

In 2015, a French court intervened and stopped parents from calling their baby daughter Nutella as it would lead to teasing or disparaging thoughts.

The parents did not attend the court hearing, so the judge ruled that their daughter would be called Ella.

*

In New Zealand, a judge ordered that a 9-year-old girl be made a ward of the court until her name was changed from "Talula Does the Hula from Hawaii". Up until that point, the girl did not tell people her real name for fear of being laughed at. Instead, she requested that they just call her "K". The judge criticised parents who give their children names like Midnight Chardonnay, Stallion, Number 16 Bus Shelter, and those that called their twins Benson and Hedges.

*

The world's largest indoor beach is the "Tropical Island Resort" in Krausnick, south of Berlin.

The former aircraft hangar, which could easily contain eight football pitches, has been transformed into a tropical escape which caters for six thousand visitors at a time. The complex, which has a constant temperature of 26°C, boasts the largest indoor pool, 50,000 plants, a spa, a waterfall, waterslides, restaurants, a cocktail bar, 400 sun loungers, and cabins which enable visitors to stay overnight.

After the company that owned the hangar went bankrupt, it was bought by a Malaysian company who saw the potential that the world's largest freestanding building had to offer. Subsequently, the beach resort opened in 2004.

*

In 1923, the famous *Hollywood* sign was erected as part of an advertising campaign for a new housing development called *Hollywood Land*.

When laws for the possession and use of marijuana were relaxed on the 1st January 1976, a prankster named Danny Finegood altered the sign to read Hollyweed. He claimed it was for a school art project for which he was given an "A".

To celebrate Easter in 1977, Finegood obscured one letter to make the sign read Holywood.

Finegood was up to his tricks again in 1987 when he altered the sign to spell out Ollywood which was in protest to the Iran-Contra scandal (a political scandal involving the sale of arms to Iran in the hope of securing hostages).

Finegood had his last fun with the sign in the early 1990s when he made the letters read "Oil War" which was a protest against the Gulf War.

At the age of 52, Finegood passed away in 2007. The cause of death was multiple myeloma.

The most recent alteration was in January 2017 when Zachary Cole Fernandez copied one of Finegood's pranks and made the sign look like Hollyweed. Although his idea was just to make people smile when they woke up in a new year, he was arrested when he turned himself in and was booked for misdemeanour trespassing.

*

Depending on the brand, and how the owner drives the vehicle, tyres supplied with a new car are expected to last for at least 50,000 miles. Once a tyre is worn out, it is usually burnt or recycled. However, in the Sulaibiya area near Kuwait City, they are dumped into one of the world's biggest landfills. At the last count, the landfill site contained over seven million tyres. The expanse of discarded rubber is so vast that it can be seen from space.

*

Exophthalmos refers to a medical condition that can cause an eyeball to protrude. One of the most common causes of exophthalmos is Grave's Disease which is a thyroid condition that causes the tissues in the eyeballs to swell and the number of cells to increase hence the eyes become bigger and are pushed forward from the socket.

The eyes are linked to the nose by cranial nerves, so when a person sneezes the stimulation travels up one nerve to the brain and along another nerve to the eyelids. This action triggers a blink for most people. Eyelids don't have a lot of muscle power, which would indicate that it is only a myth that eyes will pop out if someone sneezes while they are open.

*

Historically cannibalism has been connected to a vast range of culture-specific beliefs as well as being a way to survive a famine, to demonstrate victory after a battle, or simply to satisfy the palate that prefers human meat more than animal meat.

Exocannibalism is based on the idea that consuming flesh is a way to terrify another tribe or group of people, or to steal their life force; the act is usually associated with tribal warfare. It is practised to demonstrate superiority and disdain towards the defeated people. The Mianmin were a mountain-dwelling group living in Papua New Guinea who were renowned for practising exocannibalism after raiding neighbouring villages.

Endocannibalism is an ancient practice that involves eating the flesh of a deceased family member or someone from the same tribe. It is often done out of respect with the belief that the deceased loved one's wisdom can be absorbed. The Fore Tribe from Papua New Guinea had a protocol whereby individual family members had to eat particular body parts; each body part symbolised a unique ability or ancestral power that was passed on to the consumer.

*

Split is Croatia's second-largest city and home to the spectacular museum "Froggyland".

The museum displays over five hundred stuffed frogs divided into twenty-one exhibits which thematically arranges the frogs into various everyday life situations, e.g. frogs at school, frogs exercising, frogs rowing, frogs working in a blacksmith's forge, and frogs relaxing with a glass of wine.

Between 1910 and 1920, taxidermist Ferenc Mere recreated the human life scenes by using a taxidermy technique through the mouth so that the exhibits are devoid of any external incisions.

*

In 1974, Mike Muller, an engineer, writer, and development specialist, wrote a report for the global justice organisation "War on Want" entitled "The Baby Killer" which highlighted the horrors that infants were subjected to as a result of Nestlé's aggressive marketing strategies in the less economically developed countries of Africa, Asia, and Latin America.

Nestlé employed sales reps to dress in nurses' uniforms who then persuaded new mothers in the maternity wards to use the formula instead of breastfeeding. Free samples were distributed, but once the mothers started weaning the infants, they had no option but to buy the expensive formula. However, many could not afford it, and subsequently, the babies would go hungry. Furthermore, the product had to be mixed with water, which was often contaminated and resulted in deadly diseases.

As a result of the deaths caused by malnutrition and avoidable diseases, a global movement boycotting Nestlé took hold, and to this day, the stigma still remains.

Like many other multinational companies, Nestlé has a history of locating their production facilities in countries that have less protection for employees. Factories based in Columbia, North Korea, and China are not held to the same accountability and governance policies enabling large companies to exploit staff easier without any retribution.

*

A submarine can float because the amount of water that it displaces from its ballast tanks is equal to its weight. This water displacement creates an upward force, called the buoyant force, which acts in opposition to gravity.

A submarine is in effect two ballast tanks (or ships) with one hull inside the other. The tanks are kept afloat when the outer hull displaces water, but when it is flooded the submarine sinks, and the inner hull becomes the ship. To keep the submarine level at a set depth a balance of air and water is maintained in the ballast tanks so that the overall density is equal to the surrounding water.

To resurface, the ballast tanks are filled with compressed air forcing the water out of the submarine until the overall density is less than the surrounding water causing the submarine to rise.

Submarines are mostly equipped with a distillation apparatus that turns seawater into freshwater. The equipment can produce up to 40,000 gallons of freshwater each day, which will be used to cool electronic equipment, and by the crew for cooking, drinking, and personal hygiene.

Following an incident or other means of power failure, the crew are faced with four main dangers: -

- the ship could flood,
- oxygen could run out,
- increased carbon dioxide levels would produce toxic effects,
- the batteries that run the heating system could run out, causing the temperature to drop.

Rescue attempts must be made within 48-hours and usually involve a mini-submarine (known as a Deep-Submergence Rescue Vehicle (DSRV)) which latches over a hatch creating an airtight seal enabling twenty-four crew members to be rescued at a time.

The first known military submarine was built in 1775; it only held one crew member.

In 1870, interest in advancing submarine designs grew following the publication of "20,000 Leagues Under the Sea", written by French author, Jules Verne.

In October 2013, the residents of Milan woke one morning to find that a submarine had apparently pushed its way through the street near Via dei Mercanti. The scene was barricaded off with firefighters helping sailors escape from the submarine's tower. The ambitious publicity stunt was carried out by an Italian insurance company.

*

Some studies have shown that diet drinks can actually cause weight gain. The idea behind diet drinks is that they use artificial sweeteners to replace sugar. Test results showed that baseline sugar levels increased only slightly for the diet drinks indicating that the artificial sweeteners are successful at not raising blood sugar levels.

The reason why some studies suggest that artificial sweeteners contribute to weight gain is that the sweetener triggers a message to the brain, indicating that calories are on their way but then fails to deliver the goods. However, the sweet receptors have been triggered, and the reaction is to eat something sweet, which is laden with calories, hence the weight gain.

*

Almost everyone has heard of the five-second-rule – the idea that dropped food can be picked up and eaten if it lies on the floor no longer than five seconds (as germs wait that long before they jump on to it!).

This rule has actually been tested by scientists who found that food lying for only a few seconds collected as much as 97% of bacteria when compared to food left lying for longer. Results differ depending on the type of food involved and the type of surface that it lands on.

*

"The world Eco Garden of Butterflies and the Dwarf Empire", also known as the "Kingdom of Little People", is a theme park in China's Yunnan province. The park was founded in 2009 by real estate developer, Chen Mingjing.

The residents, who range from two feet to just over four feet tall, are ruled over by an emperor, an empress, and a parliament. Twice daily, the residents perform a variety show which includes sports, acrobatics, singing, and dancing. At other times, they can be found living inside their mushroom-shaped homes.

Controversy has shrouded the theme park which has been described as a modern-day human zoo. On the flip side of the argument, the idea was created after Mingjing saw dwarfs begging and so the creation of the park gave them shelter, employment (they can earn more than university graduates), and overall better quality of life. When their working day is completed, the park's residents return to their homes, which are specially modified dormitories designed to offer better accessibility.

*

According to the Oxford English Dictionary, the first use of the word "hello" dates to 1827 when it was used as a way to attract attention. Thomas Edison is held responsible for putting the word into everyday use as he encouraged people to answer the phone by saying "hello".

Staff at the central telephone exchanges who operated the system became known as the "hello-girls" because of their association with telephone and the greeting.

*

In Vietnam, cobra hearts are eaten as a delicacy.

The first stage of the preparation is to remove the snake's head to enable the venom to be drained into a bottle before blood is added. The heart is then removed (although it still continues to beat for a while) and dropped into a glass of the blood and venom mixture. The delicacy, which has been compared to that of an oyster, it then offered to the most distinguished dinner guest.

Cobra hearts are believed to enhance male virility.

*

White tigers are the result of generational inbreeding, but they are inclined to have various defects. The same gene that causes their coat to be white also causes the optic nerve to be wired to the wrong side of the brain which means that all white tigers are crossed eyed even if they don't look it.

*

The diameter of Mercury, the smallest planet in the solar system, is 3,032 miles (4,879 km), which is approximately 38% of the width of the Earth. The surface area is over 46 million miles^2 (about 75 million kms^2), which is around 15% of the surface area of the Earth.

A day is considered the total number of hours that it takes a planet to spin around a full rotation. For Mercury, a day lasts 1,408 hours (just over the equivalent of 58 days on earth). In comparison, a day on Mars only lasts for 25 hours.

The closest planet to the sun is Mercury.

*

Authors Charles Phillips and Alan Axelrod documented the history of recorded warfare. From the total of 1,763 wars, only 123 (i.e. 7%) were classified as occurring because of religious reasons. Historically, wars have taken place to control borders, secure trade routes, territorial conquests, or as a response to challenge political authority.

*

Exercising to music apparently increases performance by about 30%. Upbeat tunes have more information for the brain to process, which acts as a distraction making athletes less aware of their exertion.

Besides being a mood elevator, music makes people want to move. A good beat can help keep the pace, or depending on the exercise, can make the person go faster.

*

An ancient Egyptian cure for toothache was to combine mashed mouse with other ingredients to create a poultice to be applied to the infected area.

*

A documentary in 2013 revealed that Hitler was a manic-depressive hypochondriac who suffered from Parkinson's Disease and had deformed genitals. Records from his physician, Dr Theodore Morell, listed more than eighty different drugs, tonics, and treatments that were being administered, many of which contained morphine and barbiturates, along with vitamins, probiotics, bull semen, and rat poison.

Although one observer remarked that these treatments helped to keep the Führer active and alert the controversial claims generally play into the hands of Hitler-excusers who argue that as he was not of sound mind, he could not be held totally responsible for the millions of deaths that he ordered. They claim that these drugs and treatments made Hitler's bipolar disorder worse.

The reports also discussed how Hitler snorted powdered cocaine to soothe his throat and clear his sinuses as well as using eye-drops, which were infused with 10% cocaine.

Nearing the end of World War II, his rigid tactics, such as refusing to allow troops to retreat, have now been questioned and may be explained by his addiction to crystal meth.

*

John Brinkley (1885 to 1942), fraudulently claimed to be a medical doctor and operated a drug store in Milford, Kansas. After discussing potential cures for impotence with a local farmer, the pair agreed that Brinkley would surgically implant goats' testes into the farmer for a fee of $150. Brinkley performed the surgery on several clients and claimed that it was a success as babies were being conceived.

Along with other bizarre cures for medical conditions, Brinkley was earning as much as $1 million a year during the Great Depression while most of the nation was struggling.

Regardless that his ethics and reputation were questioned for many years, Brinkley managed to stay one step ahead of his enemies - that was until 1939 when he sued the American Medical Association for libel. Once he was in court, he was exposed as a fraud, and within two years was declared bankrupt.

Although he had donated generously to various charities, he is mostly remembered as the "Goat Gland Doctor".

*

The current world record holder for the world's oldest dog is held by an Australian Cattle Dog named Bluey who lived for twenty-nine years and five months (1910 to 1939) on a farm in Australia.

The unofficial record is held by another Australian dog called Maggie - an Australian Kelpie who lived on a farm for thirty years. Unfortunately, her owner lost the paperwork so Maggie could not officially be declared as the longest living dog.

For those of us over 30-years-old, we have been alive for longer than every dog in the world.

*

The "Alt" key on a keyboard is used to alternate the function of other pressed keys.

The soft reboot function operated by a keyboard is done by pressing Control, Alt, & Delete at the same time – this is known as the three-single salute.

When people verbalise the command "Alt", it is never spoken as its full title (alternate).

*

During the first series of "Friends", the numbers of the

apartments were 4 and 5. The producers realised that numbers 4 and 5 represented lower floors and had shown the friends' apartment to be much higher up. Subsequently, the apartment numbers were changed to 19 and 20.

*

Although water does not go out of date, bottled water comes with an expiration date for several reasons.

Firstly, government bureaucracy. As water is a consumable food product, it is subject to laws requiring an expiration date on all consumables. Secondly, many companies bottle water using the same machinery used to bottle other drinks. It is more cost-effective to put a date stamp on all bottles rather than dedicating another machine just for bottling water.

The expiration date is accompanied by a code which also identifies the bottling plant which is required should products need to be tracked down in the event of contamination or product recalls.

Plastic bottles do expire and eventually start to leak chemicals into the water. This will not necessarily render the water toxic, but it may lead to it having an unusual taste.

*

A *hypnagogic jerk,* commonly known as a *hypnic jerk*, is a scientific term for jumping while in the transitional period between being awake and falling asleep. It occurs when muscles twitch involuntarily and can cause the person to waken suddenly.

It is believed that the main reason for this happening is that there are two different systems in the brain battling each other - the *reticular activating system* (which keeps us awake), and the *ventrolateral preoptic nucleus* (which influences the sleep cycle). When the VPN takes over the RAS can still be partially alert – the twitches are the last attempt of the RAS to maintain control of the body.

Another theory is that as someone is drifting off to sleep, the relaxing of muscles is misinterpreted by the brain as a sign of falling and signals the muscles to tense up to protect from the potential impact.

*

If someone forgets the words or the name of a song, the website "Midomi.com" will help identify it by letting the person search by either humming or whistling the tune.

*

The founder of "Facebook", Mark Zuckerberg, is apparently red-green colour-blind which means that the colour he can see best is blue. Oddly enough, blue is the colour that dominates the "Facebook" Website.

*

The tradition of wearing a head covering, or a veil, dates back to ancient Indo-European cultures such as the Hittites, Greeks, Romans, and Persians. There was a strong association of veiling with social ranking - the Assyrian law required women of higher social ranking to wear a head covering while those of a lower social ranking, such as slaves and prostitutes, were punished if caught wearing one.

Historically, the West and Islamic cultures had two different systems, but each had similarities such as married women in Medieval Europe covering their hair with various kinds of headdresses.

Islam has continually grown since the seventh century, and as it has spread, it has incorporated some local veiling customs while having an influence on others. There are many reasons why veils are worn – for some, it can be a state requirement or a religious requirement, for others it is their culture, while some argue that Muslim women are forced to wear them. However, for immigrants in the West, they claim that the veil symbolises devotion and piety, and it is their own choice to wear them as it is their religious identity and a form of self-expression.

The four types of veils are: -

- Hijab – these veils are most popular in the West and consist of one or two scarfs that cover the head and neck.

- Niqab – this covers the entire body except for the eyes.

- Chador – this is a full body-length shawl which covers the head and the body but leaves the face completely visible.

- Burqa – this garment covers the entire body and face although there is a mesh screen covering the eyes enabling the wearer to see.

*

Doonbeg is a picturesque coastal village nestling in a sheltered bay along the Atlantic coast in West Country Clair, Ireland. One of Europe's most distinguished 5-star destinations, "Trump International Golf Links and Hotel Doonbeg", is located close to the village. The complex, which includes the world-renowned 18-hole golf course, has been named as the number two resort in Europe.

Legend has it that developers had been contemplating building on the site for over a century, but it took until 1999 before they solved the problem of access enabling construction to finally get underway.

Formerly known as "Lodge at Doonbeg", the resort was taken over in 2014 by the President Trump-owned "Trump International Golf Club Ireland Enterprises Ltd" for €15 million. A further €25 million was invested in upgrading the resort.

In total, it is reported that President Trump owns seventeen golf courses around the world. One of those is "Trump National Golf Club" in Los Angeles, California, which cost $250 million ranking it as one of the most expensive courses ever to be built.

*

A German cyclist, Jens Stötzner, set a new record in 2013 when he managed to cycle 6,708 metres underwater - the equivalent to seventy-eight laps of a swimming pool.

*

The white-tailed jackrabbit, which is native to western and central parts of North America, is actually a species of hare.

*

Ancient Egyptians used crocodile dung as a contraceptive. Dried dung was inserted into the vagina with the idea that it would soften with body temperature and form an impenetrable barrier.

*

Big Ben, also known as the Great Clock, which is located on the north side of the Houses of Parliament in Westminster, London, is one of the most famous landmarks in the world.

- Big Ben started working on the 31st of May 1859.

- The first time it chimed the hour was on the 11th of July in 1859.

- Its distinctively accurate timekeeping is maintained by a stack of coins which are placed on the pendulum to ensure a constant and steady movement of the clock's hands.

- When Parliament is in session, a light is lit above Big Ben.

- Big Ben is owned by tax-paying citizens in the U.K.

- Big Ben chimes in the key of E.

In 1949, a flock of birds perched on the minute hand and caused the clock to slow down by approximately five minutes.

Snow caused the clock to slow down by ten minutes during the winter of 1962.

*

The world's smallest independent republic is the Republic of Nauru (formerly known as Pleasant Island) – an island country located 26 miles south of the equator in the southwestern Pacific Ocean.

Nauru is the least visited country in the world (only two

hundred people visited in 2011), but for those that do visit, they may be able to watch the traditional sport of lassoing flying birds as they return from foraging at sea. Any captured birds are kept and roosted as pets.

The residents of Nauru rank as the most obese in the world.

*

Although the urban meaning of *to bite down* is connected to drugs and alcohol, the traditional definition is to grip or tear with teeth or the jaw.

A normal bite and jaw joint work together; when the mouth opens, the jawbone rotates in the joint but stays braced against the skull. When the mouth is closed again, the jaw rises back upwards until all teeth come into contact at the same time. So, quite literally, you cannot actually bite down on anything – you bite up.

Corrective jaw surgery is a bone cutting procedure that involves realigning the upper and lower jaws. However, as with all operations, it comes with risks which can include permanent facial numbness or even paralysis. Yet, in spite of this, and the fact that recovery can take months, South Koreans have been encouraged to undergo the procedure in the name of beauty. A face that has a "V" shaped chin and jaw is categorised as feminine beauty. The craze has not been without problems, though as 52% have experienced sensory issues. One 23-year-old committed suicide after she was left unable to chew food or stop crying due to nerve damage in a tear duct.

*

Toilet phobias can be caused by factors such as anxiety, a bad experience, or trauma, but they can also be a learnt behaviour.

Paruresis, also known as *bashful bladder*, is a social anxiety disorder that affects around four million men and women in the U.K., and twenty-one million Americans. The most common symptom of the condition is when a man is unable to urinate at a urinal if there are other men close by. The reason it happens is that there is an involuntary neurological shutdown of the sphincter valve that usually opens to allow urine to flow freely.

Parcopresis, often called *bashful bowel*, is known medically as *Psychogenic Faecal Retention*, which is the inability to defecate when other people may be around. While it is natural to want privacy for such a private bodily function, the reaction can become over-exaggerated if someone is unable to use toilet facilities even when the need is urgent.

When serving on a Chicago jury in 2004, it was reported that Oprah Winfrey could not use the bathroom attached to the jury room unless her fellow jurors sang Kumbaya to drown out any potentially embarrassing noises.

Freud believed that developing control over the bladder and bowel movement led to a sense of accomplishment and independence. He thought that praise from parents encouraged positive outcomes and helped children feel capable and productive, which would later serve as a foundation for people to become competent, productive, and creative. However, should a toilet accident result in punishment, ridicule, or shame, the outcome could be harmful, whereby the individual could develop negative personality qualities.

The first self-cleaning public toilet was installed in Madison Square Park, New York. After use, there is a 90-second period during which time a sweeping arm sprays disinfectant, the floor is cleaned with seven gallons of water, and the place is dried by a blast of hot air. Service users have a maximum of fifteen minutes before an alarm sounds, and the door bursts wide-open automatically. Let's hope there is not a malfunction when someone with a bashful bladder or bashful bowel is using it!

*

Terrance Stanley Fox (1958 – 1981) discovered at the age of eighteen that he had a malignant tumour in his right leg which lead to an amputation fifteen centimetres above the knee. The night before the surgery, he learned of an amputee runner, which gave him encouragement and a goal.

In April 1980, Fox began running twenty-six miles each day across Canada. Leaving from St John's, Newfoundland, he arrived just outside Ontario 143 days later – in total, he ran 3,339 miles. Fox's hope to raise $1 from every Canadian to help fight cancer was achieved in 1981 when the "Terry Fox Marathon of Hope" had funds of $24.17 million. Fox died five months later at the age of 22.

*

The Santa Maria Volcano is a large active volcano in the Western Highlands of Guatemala. The volcano had been dormant for over five-hundred years when it erupted in October 1902. After lying dormant for a further twenty years, it erupted again and has continued to erupt almost every hour for the past ninety-five years. Scientists believe that there is a magma supply at depth, which is feeding the volcano and creating small yet continuous explosions.

The word volcano originally comes from *Vulcan,* which was the name of the Roman God of Fire.

The world's tallest volcano is Mauna Kea. When measured from its base on the ocean floor to the summit, it stands at over 30,000 feet tall. This Hawaiian volcano is also the world's tallest mountain.

The largest volcano in the solar system is Olympus Mons located on Mars. At an estimated 13 to 16 miles (21-27 km) in height, it is between 2.5 to 3 times taller than Mount Everest.

*

The art of sword swallowing was introduced in India around 4,000 years ago by fakirs and shaman priests. It was created as part of a demonstration of power and to show a connection to the gods.

It can take some people between three to seven years to learn how to master the art; it is usually a family tradition and therefore taught by a father to his son. Psychologically it takes years of practice as well as the need to develop a strong mind-over-matter attitude which enables the person to consciously relax both the mind and the body.

As the blade slides down the throat, it is within an eighth of an inch from several internal organs as it passes the heart and lungs en route to the stomach. When it is retracted, a nasty taste of metal and stomach acids can be left in the mouth. Veronica Hernandez from Knox City, Texas, became the first sword swallower to continue her act even when she was nine months pregnant.

"World Sword Swallower's Day" was first celebrated in 2008 and continues to the present time to promote the art, to educate people about the contributions sword swallowers have made to medicine and science, to raise funds for oesophagal cancer research, and to teach sword-swallowing pupils the skills required to perform.

*

Île de Ré is an island off the west coast of France which is home to the Poitou Donkey - a breed easily recognisable by its large size, shaggy coat, and the fact that every morning it is custom for the locals to dress the donkeys in pyjamas. There is a good reason for this practice though as the pyjamas help keep mosquitoes and other insects from biting their legs.

*

Hans Christian Andersen's story of "The Little Mermaid" told of a crueller deal that was made between the mermaid, Ariel, and the Sea Witch, which is very different from the arrangement portrayed in the Disney film. Originally Ariel agreed that the witch could take her tongue in exchange for legs even though every single step she took would feel like walking on sharp shards of glass.

At first, it seemed like the plan was working as she found the prince she had saved from drowning. However, he had plans to marry another whom he thought was the person who had saved him. To makes matters worse, the mermaid had no tongue, so she was not able to tell the prince who she really was. At this point, the only way Ariel could return to her previous life was by killing the prince, but as she was still in love with him, she decided instead to throw herself into the sea where she turned into sea foam.

*

An ostrich's eye is approximately the size of a snooker ball. It measures about two inches in diameter and is larger than the size of its brain. It is the largest eye of any land mammal.

Ostriches can grow as tall as nine feet making them the biggest bird in the world.

Their lifespan can range between 50 to 75 years.

They lay the largest eggs – it takes two hours to boil one (a long wait for breakfast!). The eggshell is so strong that it can hold the weight of a full-grown man.

Each foot has only two toes. Their feet have a strong enough impact to kill a lion or a cheetah with one kick.

In the 1800s, people used ostrich feathers for making clothes. They were hunted so much for this reason that they almost became extinct.

Their feathers are unlike the feathers of other birds as they do not produce oils. They are designed for the extreme living conditions they are exposed to - as the temperature rises during the day the air circulates through the feathers whereas during the cold nights the feathers are retracted closer to the body and act as an insulator.

The ostrich has the most powerful immune system of any animal.

*

Celebrating a child's tooth falling out has been a long-standing universal tradition. As far back as the 13th century, a Middle Eastern custom was to throw baby-teeth into the air while praying for a better tooth to replace it.

To encourage a new tooth to grow, children in Greece, India, and Korea, would traditionally have thrown teeth from the upper jaw onto the ground, while teeth from the lower jaw were throw up into the air as it was believed this action would make new teeth grow strong. Other traditions ranged from hiding a tooth in a mouse hole, placing it in a tree, or for the child or its mother to swallow the tooth.

Not all traditions were as much fun. Finnish and Norwegian children were warned about the tooth troll who would come to take them away if they did not brush their teeth.

One tale that has remained predominant around the world is that of the mouse who comes to collect any teeth that have fallen out – if the child has also left out some cheese the mouse may exchange the tooth for a present or some money.

The earliest reference to the tooth fairy appeared in the "Chicago Tribune" in 1908. It is thought that it was a cross-pollination of two fictional figures – the mouse, and the good fairy. The story was further popularised by a children's story entitled "The Tooth Fairy" which was written by Esther Watkins Arnold in 1927.

It has been argued that the tooth fairy serves as a much-needed source of comfort as losing a tooth can be a daunting experience for a young child; it is deemed as the first rite of passage. A monetary reward helps children transition into the world of adulthood where cash is perceived as a symbol of responsibility.

"National Tooth Fairy Day" is held on the 28th February and on the 22nd August, each year.

Human adults have thirty-two teeth in total – eight incisors, four canines, eight premolars, and twelve molars (which include four wisdom teeth).

The most valuable tooth once belonged to Sir Isaac Newtown. In 1816, it was sold in London for £730 (which was the equivalent of approximately £50k today) to an aristocrat who had it set in a ring.

In November 2011, John Lennon's tooth was sold at auction for a final hammer price of £19,500 (plus £3,510 auction house commission); it is officially titled as the most expensive tooth sold at auction.

*

The centrepiece of any presidential motorcade is the president's limousine. The vehicle that was used for the inauguration of President Trump was in development for many years and had an estimated (but unconfirmed) $15 million spent on research and development alone. During the development stage, the car was covered in camouflage paint to disguise its new features.

The limousine is officially known as the *presidential state car,* but more often than not, it is referred to as *the beast.* The vehicle comes equipped with eight-inch-thick armoured doors (that weight the same as the door of a Boeing 747), and bulletproof glass that can stop a .44 magnum bullet. The body of the vehicle is made up of five inches of military-grade armour, and the floor has armoured plates that will withstand grenades and bombs thrown underneath it. If the fuel tank is punctured, there is a special foam that will seal it to deter any explosion. The tyres are reinforced with Kevlar (a high-strength synthetic fibre) and are shred and puncture-resistant; they also have steel rims enabling the car to make a get-away even if the tyres are blasted away.

Some extras that the beast can boast about are its night vision cameras, tear gas cannons, pump-action shotguns, and fire-fighting equipment. The car also comes furnished with a supply of oxygen to enable the President to survive a chemical attack, as well as two pints of blood matching the President's blood type.

The maximum speed the beast can travel at is 60 mph, but the chauffeur is a specially trained Secret Service agent who can handle the car through nearly any situation if the need arises.

It is believed that there are around twelve presidential limousines at any given time - one reason for having so many is that there are usually two or three used at any presidential motorcade. Although the other beasts may be used to transport VIP's they are more often than not used as decoys. Before the President makes an official trip, one of his limousines is sent ahead, which is another reason why more than one vehicle is required.

The question has been asked why President J.F. Kennedy was travelling in an open-top presidential state car on the day he was shot. Several theories have arisen with one being that a presidential vehicle would have been impersonal as the aim of his visit to Dallas was to win over a city that had lingering hostility towards him. Another theory is that while it was recognised that the people of Dallas had not been won over by the president, they did have a love for his wife, so perhaps he had wanted to show her off.

*

Some people view world records as an achievement while others see them as a target to exceed (even if they set it!).

In 2007, an Indian thrill-seeker, Sailendra Nath Roy, zip-lined from one building to another using his ponytail. A year later he managed to pull the famous Darjeeling Toy Train (which weighs more than forty tonnes) for 8.2 feet by his ponytail. Although he set the Guinness Book of World Records for travelling the furthest distance on a zip wire by using his ponytail in 2011, he decided to try to beat it two years later by crossing a six-hundred-foot-long zip-wire at the height of seventy feet above the Teesta River in West Bengal. Halfway through the stunt he came to a halt and for half an hour desperately tried to get his ponytail untangled. Suddenly his arms fell to his sides, and he became totally limp. After hanging for a total of forty-five minutes, he was brought down and rushed to the hospital; he was pronounced dead on arrival, having suffered a massive heart attack.

*

On 2nd December 1959, following five days of strong winds and heavy rain on the French Riviera, the Malpasset Dam in Conn, France, burst without warning. Tonnes of water cascaded down on the town of Fréjus ripping homes from their foundations and burying people in the mud – others were swept out to sea. The death toll came to about five-hundred people.

President Charles de Gaulle visited the area following the aftermath and was approached by a young, grieving woman who asked if she could posthumously marry her fiancé who was among those who had perished. Subsequently, a new law was passed, which granted her her heart's desire.

The law of posthumous marriages still exists providing permission is granted by the president and that the deceased's family give their approval. It is a symbolic marriage, and there is no financial reward other than that already bequeathed.

*

The word "swastika" comes from the Sanskrit (an ancient Indo-Aryan language) word *svástika* which means *good fortune*. The motif was used thousands of years ago in Neolithic Eurasia and is still a sacred symbol in Buddhism, Hinduism, Jainism, and Odinism.

At the beginning of the 20th century, the swastika was used throughout Europe as a symbol of good luck and auspiciousness before it was adopted by the Germans as a symbol of nationalist pride. After World War I some far-right nationalist movements adopted the swastika, and it became known as a symbol of a racially pure state. By the time the Nazis had gained control of Germany, the connotations of the emblem had changed forever.

*

Many years after his death, Alan Turing (1912 to 1954) became famous and is known today as the father of theoretical computer science and artificial intelligence.

During the Second World War, he devised several techniques to speed up the process of breaking German cyphers. He played a pivotal role in cracking intercepted coded messages that enabled the Allies to defeat the Nazis in many critical engagements. As a computer scientist, mathematician, and cryptanalyst, he was able to decrypt the Enigma machine which had been designed by the German engineer, Arthur Scherbius, to send coded information securely. The cracking of the Enigma code was accredited with shortening the war and saving countless lives.

Following the war, Turing designed what would today be considered as a digital computer which stored programs in its memory. Alongside that, he also issued a report detailing software issues and predicted future non-numeric applications of computers.

In 1967, Turing was prosecuted for having an affair with another man. Rather than face prison, he accepted probation on the condition that he would be chemically castrated. His security clearance was revoked, which terminated his work in the governments code-breaking department; he was barred from continuing his cryptographic consultancy for the government. To escape British law, Turing moved to Norway and then on to Greece.

On the 8th June 1954, Turing was found dead. An inquest determined that he had committed suicide. However, his mother believed that his death was accidental, but others theorise that Turing orchestrated his death to look accidental on his mother's account.

In December 2013, Turing was granted a posthumous royal pardon which formally cancelled his criminal conviction. The petition calling for Turing's posthumous pardon reached 37,000 signatures and was supported by scientists Stephen Hawking and Richard Dawkins.

*

There are at least one hundred different types of cabbage grown throughout the world. China is the greatest manufacture while Russia consumes the most. It can be used for medicinal purposes such as the treatment of intestinal ulcers, engorged breasts, sore throats, rheumatism, and can also be used as a laxative. Cabbage is up to 93% water and has a powerful diuretic benefit.

*

According to widely circulated reports in 1947/1948, many ships in the trade route of the straits of Malacca picked up a series of SOS signals from a vessel known as the Ourang Medan. Due to the urgency in the distress message, the captain and crew of the Silver Star headed towards the ship requiring assistance.

As the Silver Star neared the Ourang Medan, the crew noticed that there was not any sign of life on deck. Upon boarding the ill-fated ship, the Silver Star's crew found dead bodies strewn everywhere - the eyes and mouth on all the bodies were wide open with the faces twisted into visages of agony and horror.

In an attempt to tow the ship back to port a tow line was attached. However, the rescue team noticed billows of smoke blasting up from the lower decks, in particular from the Number 4 hold. With scarcely enough time to cut the towline, the Ourang Medan exploded before swiftly sinking.

Many theories surround the event which includes the idea that there was an invasion of the paranormal, or that methane rose quickly from the ocean floor and consequently poisoned the crew.

Researchers and historians continuously come to a dead-end when trying to solve the mystery. The major stumbling block was the fact that no official documents existed for the Dutch freighter. Professor Theodor Siersdorfer pursued the case for the best part of fifty years. One piece of evidence that he did discover hinted that the Number 4 hold may have contained exceedingly harmful and highly illegal substances which might explain the demise of the crew and the subsequent explosion. The contents might have been on their way to a laboratory where they were to be used in the development of chemical and biological weapons. This reason would explain why the ship's paperwork could not be found as it would have been an embarrassment to any government.

Since there were not any crew members to come forward to tell the tale, many believe that it was all a hoax. Regardless of whether it was true or not, it has still remained one of the most frightening maritime stories to date.

*

Central Hypoventilation Syndrome, also known as Ondine's Curse, requires the afflicted to consciously focus on breathing all the time. This rare lifelong and life-threatening disorder affects the central and autonomic nervous system which controls many of the body's automatic functions such as the heart rate, blood pressure, bowel and bladder control, and the sensing of oxygen and carbon dioxide levels in the blood. It is estimated that there are between 1,000 to 1,200 sufferers worldwide.

The most recognised symptom is the inability to control breathing which can result in the need for life-long ventilator support while sleeping; bedtime is particularly dangerous as without the essential breathing support the person would simply stop breathing and never wake up.

In a French folktale written by Friedrich de la Motte Foaqué, Ondine was a nymph who was a water goddess of extreme beauty. Humans were a danger to nymphs and should the two species ever marry the nymph would lose her eternal youthfulness and begin to age. However, Ondine met and married Palemon and together they had a son. As Ondine's youthful beauty began to fade, Palemon rekindled his relationship with his first-love, Berta, whom he had previously been engaged to before he met Ondine. When Ondine found out about his affair, she was consumed with anger and regret. With just enough magic left, she cursed her husband so that if he ever fell asleep, his breathing would stop.

*

The bacterial infection, Syphilis, is generally transmitted through sexual contact. Symptoms include sores, ulcers, a blotchy red rash, white patches in the mouth, as well as tiredness, headaches, joint pain, and swollen glands. A course of antibiotics will usually cure the problem, but if it is left untreated, it can spread to the brain and cause serious long-term problems.

Al Capone (1899 to 1947) was promoted to leader of Chicago's underworld organisation when he was twenty-six years old. From many illicit activities, which included bootlegging, gambling, and prostitution, his gang pulled in an estimated $100 million a year. Although the authorities knew about his actions, he avoided prosecution for years by keeping some police officers and other officials on his payroll, and by threatening witnesses. In 1931, the government were finally able to charge him with income-tax fraud, and he was fined $50,000 as well as being sentenced to serve eleven years' imprisonment (during which time he was transferred to Alcatraz).

During his time in prison, Capone's behaviour changed. He reportedly mumbled to himself and talked like a baby; he would often hunker down in the corner of his jail cell, and he failed to recognise people that he knew. At first, it was thought that the experience had broken him, but it was soon discovered that his brain was being eaten away due to advanced syphilis which he had contracted at the age of 18.

After being released, Capone spent his last years on his estate in Miami where he would sit for hours beside the swimming pool with his fishing rod hoping to catch imaginary fish. His physician stated that he had the mental capacity of a 12-year-old.

Despite Capone's imprisonment, and all the other efforts that the government made to reduce bootlegging, the flow of liquor into Chicago never even slowed down.

*

The first porn movie was made it 1896. The seven-minute French film was entitled "Le Coucher de la Mariée" (which translates as "Bedtime for the Bride") and it showed a woman performing a striptease in the bathroom before she had a bath and got dressed again. Today, all that remains of the silent movie is the first ninety seconds.

*

Although many believe that one of the Founding Fathers of the U.S.A., Benjamin Franklin, invented the rocking chair, no one really knows who the creator was. Franklin was only a young child when they first appeared.

*

Mount Edgecumbe is a dormant volcano situated in Kruzof Island, Alaska. On the morning of Monday 1st April 1974, the residents of Sitka woke up to see black smoke plummeting from the crater and thought that the volcano was preparing to blow.

Hours earlier, 50-year-old Oliver Bickar, accompanied by fellow pranksters, had flown seventy tyres up to the crater. Along with smoke bombs, gallons of kerosene, and some rags, the tyres were set alight before the gang fled the scene.

Precautions had been taken to warn local authorities to ensure there was no real panic. The prank went on record as one of the all-time best April Fool's jokes. News of it got picked up by the press, and it ran in papers around the world.

*

Every year about six million people visit the Musée du Louvre in Paris to gaze at what is most likely the world's most famous painting - the Mona Lisa. The identity of the person who posed for the artwork has been shrouded in mystery – some claim that there were various models used while others think that it was actually a portrait of a male model. However, it is widely speculated that the Mona Lisa is a portrait of Lisa del Giocondo, who was the wife of a wealthy Florentine silk merchant.

After years of examining the remains of bodies buried below the Sant'Orsola convent in Florence, Italian researchers thought they had found the bones of Lisa del Giocondo, who died in 1542 at the age of 63. However, as the remains were limited (the skull was missing), it has been impossible to finally conclude whether it was del Giocondo or not.

Although a consensus emerged in 2005 when a 500-year-old note by a government clerk was discovered that claimed del Giocondo was the subject of the painting, researchers are likely going to have to wait for a few more years to conclude the accuracy of this claim as the required DNA technology has not yet been invented.

Leonardo da Vinci had two students paint their own version of the Mona Lisa at the same time. One is called the *Prado Mona Lisa* after the Spanish museum that it is displayed in. Historians and researchers suggest that the painting was made by a copyist in da Vinci's studio at precisely the same time the original was painted.

The other version was of a topless Mona Lisa and had remained hidden for almost a century within the panelled walls of the private library of Cardinal Joseph Fesch, Napoleon's ambassador to the Vatican. Experts think that this may be da Vinci's own work as it has mostly been done by a left-handed artist (although they agree they may never be absolutely sure about its origins).

Following Leonardo da Vinci's death, King Francis I of France hung the Mona Lisa in his bathroom - a six-roomed bathing suite where the king and his guests smoked, soaked, and sweated.

*

The Cairn de Barnenez (which is referred to as Barnenez Mound or Barnenez Tumulus) is a prehistoric monument located in Brittany, France. The first phase of construction is dated from 4,850 B.C. to 4,500 B.C., and the second phase began in 4,200 B.C., indicating that it is two-thousand years older than the Great Pyramid of Giza.

It measures 236 feet long, between 65 and 83 feet wide, and 29 feet tall.

The cairn was actually used as a quarry until the middle of the twentieth century. It was at that point that the monuments archaeological value was realised, and excavation and restoration work began.

This megalithic building is considered as the oldest building in the world as well as one of the very first buildings in Europe.

*

In 2012, just eight years after Facebook had been created, thirty million of its users had died. Some estimates suggest that more than eight-thousand users die daily. If the popularity of the platform takes a dip, it is estimated that there will come the point in time that the majority of its 1.5 billion users will actually be dead. Statisticians debate what year this will occur, but the earliest suggestion is 2065.

*

Ear wax, which is scientifically known as cerumen, has natural antibacterial properties and is produced to protect ears from infections, dust, bacteria, and other micro-organisms.

Genetics create two different types of earwax: -

- dry earwax, which is made up of 18% fat and 43% protein, and
- wet earwax, which contains about 50% fat and 20% protein.

*

Ellen Kelly was born in County Antrim, Ireland in 1832. Nine years later her family emigrated to Australia where she met and married John "Red" Kelly – a convict who had been sentenced to Australia for theft.

As a widowed mother of twelve children (to three different men) it was her eldest son, Ned (who later became Australia's most notorious outlaw), who became the undeclared head of the family when he was just 12-years-old. With the stress of being a single parent to so many and the struggle to make a living from inferior farmland, Ellen became notorious for her violent temper, which resulted in various court appearances.

Her son Dan was in the horse-thieving business, but when the police tried to arrest him, Ellen was blamed for attacking the constable resulting in her being charged with attempted murder. Although she always denied the incident and pleaded innocent, she was sentenced to three years' imprisonment.

The night before Ned's execution, Ellen was allowed to visit but was shocked to see the grimness in his face. Apparently, the last words Ellen said to her son were "mind you die like a Kelly, son".

While in prison, the woman once branded as a notoriously bad woman became known as a model prisoner and later a respected member of the community.

On her release, Ellen was left to raise some of her grandchildren as seven of her twelve children died. Ellen passed away in 1923 at the age of 91.

While one son had become Australia's most infamous outlaw, another, Jack Kelly, became a highly-decorated policeman and a worldwide star on the rodeo circuit.

*

In an interview in March 2017, Ed Sheeran was asked what was the worst injury that he had ever suffered. He replied that it was the time when he put his foot in a pool of boiling water when he was climbing up a volcano.

*

John Edwards is a former drug addict and alcoholic who has been sober for more than two decades. He described the turning point in his life as an incredible encounter with God after which he set up a Christian rehabilitation centre and homeless shelter.

Originally from Dublin, Ireland, Edwards continually seeks to find new and innovative ways to reach out to people. In March 2017, he was buried alive for three days in the graveyard of Willowfield Church in Belfast. The event was broadcast live on social media and Edwards communicated with members of the public by receiving phone calls, texts, and emails. His message from the grave was to raise awareness of addiction and suicide and to extend the message of hope by trusting in God.

The coffin, measuring 8 feet long by 3.5 feet high, and 4 feet wide, was specially adapted and equipped with a portable toilet, ventilation, and had access to food and water supplies.

Word spread as far as China where it was even broadcast on the news.

*

Gloria Ramirez (1963 to 1994) was a California woman who was dubbed as *The Toxic Lady* due to events leading up to her death.

Ramirez, who had been diagnosed with metastatic cervical cancer sometime earlier, was rushed to hospital in respiratory and cardiac distress. Approximately fifteen minutes after her arrival, she went into full cardiac arrest. Following standard "code blue" procedures, a nurse took a blood sample but on doing so noticed a foul odour and passed out. Immediately after that, all staff within close proximity collapsed.

The emergency department was sealed, patients were evacuated, and the decontamination unit was ushered in. Attempts to resuscitate Ramirez failed, and she was pronounced dead about forty-five minutes later.

Investigations into the event took nine months to complete at which time it was concluded that the cause of death was that the chemical warfare agent, Dimethyl Sulfate, had been created by an unusual confluence of chemical reactions. One theory is that when the paramedics administered oxygen, it mixed with dimethyl sulfoxide (which the patient had been prescribed to help relieve various arthritic pains) to become dimethyl sulfone. Then, when the nurse drew a sample of blood, the dimethyl sulfone experienced a quick change in temperature, thus creating dimethyl sulfate.

There are other theories too, one of which is that Ramirez had been abducted by aliens and chemical reactions were as a result of extra-terrestrial experiments.

Some of the staff who had been affected spent several weeks in hospital as they developed shortness of breath, involuntary muscle spasms, and loss of consciousness.

Sadly, Ramirez is remembered as the Toxic Lady and not the 31-year-old woman who lost the battle with cancer and is buried in an unmarked grave.

*

Mauro Prosperi (b. 1955) was 39 years old when he took part in the 1994 "Marathon des Sables" – a six-day 155-mile (c 250 km) race through the Sahara.

On the fourth day, the Italian runner found himself battling a storm and eventually found a sheltered spot to wait for the storm to pass. Eight hours later, he surfaced to discover a transformed landscape. He immediately realised that he had no idea where he was exactly or what direction to head, so he began to take survival precautions which started with urinating in his spare water bottle to help with dehydration. After a few days of wandering, he came across a marabout (a Muslim shrine) where he was able to take shelter. Inside he was accompanied by a holy man in a coffin, and some bats hanging in the tower. Capturing twenty of the bats, he cut their heads off, mushed up their insides with a knife, and sucked them out.

Frustrated that a helicopter and aeroplane flew over without spotting him, Prosperi decided that suicide was his only option. However, when his wrists were cut, the blood would not drain as it had thickened. With that plan crossed off the list, he woke up the next morning and headed towards the clouds on the horizon (advice given to him before the race). On the eighth day after getting lost, he found an oasis where he was able to get a fresh supply of water. The following day he was found by a young shepherd girl and eventually rescued. He was 181 miles off course, suffered liver damage, and it took almost two years for him to fully recover.

Four years later he was back at Marathon des Sables and has completed it eight times since.

*

According to records of the 9/11 terrorist attack on the World Trade Centre, there were twenty survivors pulled alive from the rubble. Genelle Guzman-McMillan was the last person to be pulled out alive after waiting twenty-seven hours before being found.

Sixty-one foreign countries were affected; Britain had the second-largest loss of life, accounting for 67 people from a total of 372 foreign nationals.

Most of the 185,101 tons of metal left at Ground Zero was recycled with the majority of it being shipped to China and India. The rest was used as material to create memorials across all fifty states.

*

Nagoro, which is also known as Nagoro Scarecrow Village, lies on the island of Shikoku in Tokushima Prefecture, Japan. In August 2016, the remote mountainous area had a population of just thirty people.

Japanese artist, Tsukimi Ayano, moved back to the village to care for her elderly father. After he passed away, Ayano made a scarecrow for the garden, which was meant to resemble her father doing something that he enjoyed. This gave her the idea that she could repopulate the village with dolls/scarecrows that looked like former residents.

Ten years later, the scarecrow population had increased to 350 with each individual strategically placed where Ayano recalled seeing the actual living person. The village has become a tourist attraction where visitors can see the creations either working in the fields, sitting at the river fishing, positioned at the roadside carrying out essential maintenance, learning at school, or simply relaxing on their front porch.

Check it out on Google Earth!

*

An element is a substance that can not be broken down any further.

Antoine-Laurent de Lavoisier (1743 to 1794), a French nobleman and a chemist, wrote the first extensive list of elements and published a paper which set forward the theory of elements. However, it was a Russian chemist called Dmitri Mendeleev whose version was adopted as he used a method of predicting the existence of substances which, at that time, were still not discovered.

Legend has it that Mendeleev was utterly exhausted by the conundrum of trying to sort the elements into an order that he fell asleep and had a dream in which he saw in front of him a table where all the elements fell into place as required. When he woke up, he wrote down the design which revealed a hidden periodic pattern.

The way to establish if something is an element or not is to conduct experiments on it, e.g. heating the object to see what wavelengths of light come out of it or to put different voltages of electricity through it to observe how the current changes.

Ytterby is a village on the small island of Resarö in the Stockholm archipelago, which has benefitted economically from a mine which contained feldspar – a product used to make Chinese porcelain. Anything else that the miners found was dumped into a refuse heap, but soon geologists and chemists heard stories about the rare minerals turning up in Ytterby and began experimenting with them. Seven new elements were eventually discovered; four of them were given names after the village where they were found – *ytterbium, yttrium, terbium,* and *erbium.* Two were named after Stockholm, i.e. *holmium,* and *thulium,* while the last was named *gadolinium* after the Finnish chemist Johan Gadolin.

Ytterby is the only place in the world where four new elements were found and the only place that has elements named after it. It is also the only place in the world with streets named after elements which makes knowledge of the periodic table useful for getting around town.

*

Infrasound is any soundwave under 20 hertz that can make the listener feel various emotions - it is like a deep bassline in music which can physically affect a person by making them have goosebumps or think that they feel the presence of someone standing beside them.

The use of infrasound has become more frequent amongst film producers in a bid to manipulate the viewer into experiencing the movies' events to the full. This is especially evident in horror movies which historically relied on orchestral scores to fill in the silence and create an atmosphere. Now with infrasound, the horror-movie underscore can cause a more direct sense of danger, making the audience become a passive participant. Infrasound induces anxiety, extreme sorrow, heart palpitations, and shivering.

The 2002 French movie "Irréversible" was a psychological horror film that followed two men through the streets of Paris as they sought to avenge a brutally raped girlfriend. An American film critic warned that the movie was so violent and cruel that most people would probably find it unwatchable. His prediction was correct as a lot of viewers headed for the cinema exit within a short time of the movie beginning. However, this wasn't necessarily because of what was seen on screen but because, as explained by the director Gaspar Noé, a 27-Hz frequency of bass had been used to induce panic and anxiety.

The 2007 horror movie "Paranormal Activity" used a similar technique which also led to viewers rushing out of the movie theatre because they were so frightened.

*

The American actor, James Dean, was the first actor to receive a posthumous "Academy Award" nomination for best actor. To date, he is the only actor to have had two posthumous nominations.

*

Voodoo originated in Africa and is described as a blend of magical and religious practices that takes on different characteristics depending on the location it is being practised.

There are three variations and each draw on the culture

around it: -

- West African voodoo is still practised by an estimated 30 million people and is the version that remains mostly untouched by outside influences.

- Louisiana Voodoo has been heavily influenced by the practices of the Creole population as well as by French and Spanish Settlers.

- Haitian Voodoo (also known as Vodou) has been shaped by French influence, but it has also taken on some practices from Christianity. An alliance was formed with the Catholic Church when Pope John Paul II attended a Voodoo ceremony in 1993.

Rada Voodoo is viewed as a peaceful practice, while Petro is considered as a more dangerous version. Although those that practise Voodoo do not think of it as either black or white magic, they do refer to the dark element as *red* magic because when a practitioner allows an evil spirit to take possession, their eyes turn red.

A former chemistry student in New York, Max Beauvoir (1936 to 2015), had a promising career planned out as a biochemist when his grandfather passed away. On his death bed, the grandfather unexpectedly anointed Beauvoir as his successor as a houngan – a voodoo priest. As a result, Beauvoir left his career behind and dedicated his life to Voodooism. He was elected by Haiti's houngans as the Supreme Chief for the newly formed National Confederation of Haitian Vodou. During his lifetime, he lobbied for official recognition for the houngans as healers. He also sought to transform Hollywood's image from that of "shaman with suspicious practices" to that of priests who bond body and soul together and welcome the idea of reincarnation.

Beauvoir founded the "Peristyle of Marian", a voodoo temple which doubled as a medical clinic and research centre.

Since the religious syncretism between the Catholic Church and Vodou, it is difficult to estimate the number of Vodouists in Haiti.

A female priest is referred to as a *mambo*.

*

Carol Ann Doda (1937 to 2015) was the first dancer to appear topless in public in San Francisco's Condo Club. In September 1969 Doda began dancing in the nude until a rule was passed in 1972 prohibiting naked dancing in places that served alcohol.

*

A *Google Doodle* is a temporary alteration to the Google logo visible on the search engine's homepage. It is intended to celebrate events, achievements, people, and other special occasions.

Google began in 1996 as a research project for two students at Stanford University – Larry Page and Sergey Brin. Less than one week before Google officially became incorporated as a company, they both decided to attend the "Burning Man" festival. As a way to let people know that they were *out-of-the-office,* they added a stick figure to the Google logo – the idea of decorating the company logo to celebrate significant events was born. Since then, more than two thousand doodles have been created for homepages around the world.

*

There is an area covering approximately 39 miles^2 (101 kms^2) in France (in comparison, Paris is 40.7 miles^2 (105.4 kms^2)) from which the public is strictly prohibited due to the vast number of unexploded chemical weaponry that have yet to be recovered from the battlefields of both World Wars.

Known as "Zone Rouge" (the Red Zone) the once well-maintained village and farmland district became an unrecognisable dense forest. Until 2004 the area was regularly used by hunters until it was discovered that the arsenic level in the soil was hazardous – it had actually increased by tens-of-thousands compared to the levels previously recorded. Water was infected by 300 times the tolerated amount and hunters discovered that wild boars had damaged livers as a result. The Authorities finally prohibited access to the area in 2012.

During the early stages of the "clean-up", thousands of bombs were destroyed without taking into consideration the effect that this would have on the ground and water. Scattered debris contaminated the soil with lead, mercury, and zinc; it is reckoned that these elements will continue to pollute the area for at least another 10,000 years.

Contamination aside, optimistic experts believe that at the current rate of clean-up it could take anywhere between 300 to 700 years to complete the clearance work while others argue that it will never be fully completed.

*

The colossal squid can grow up to 46 feet in length and has eyes that measure approximately 27 cms across (which are comparable to the size of a football). Its eyes are considered to be the largest in the animal kingdom.

*

Bears are the only animals that do not urinate nor defecate during hibernation. The shorter days on the run-up to hibernation trigger biological changes which help the animals to prepare for the event. During the five to seven months of hibernation, the bears' intestinal secretions and cells start to slough off and form a plug which can expand up to 15 inches long in diameter. This plug is basically faecal matter that has remained in the intestine for so long that the intestinal walls have absorbed the fluids leaving it hard and dry.

On examination, the plugs also contain hair and plant material which can be explained by the fact that bears tend to groom themselves during hibernation. As they groom, they lick fragments of bedding (such as leaves, grass, and tree bark) off their fur which passes through the digestive tract unchanged. Also, the calloused soles of their feet shed, and as this happens, they are inclined to lick their tender feet ingesting pieces of the pads.

This activity does open up the question, though whether bears have "true" hibernations.

*

Although the first sperm donation took place in Philadelphia in 1884, there was little record of its success nor were detailed reports available for procedures that took place during the next sixty years.

In 1945, the "British Medical Journal" published the first modern account of sperm donation. However, the research paper, which had been submitted by Dr Mary Barton, was regarded by the majority as controversial and resulted with politicians and church leaders around the world calling for donor insemination to be made illegal. However, although the Pope deemed it as a sin, and the Archbishop of Canterbury called for Parliament to make the procedure illegal, there was not any action taken which left it neither legal nor illegal.

For the next 25-years, couples who conceived by artificial insemination kept it a private matter. That was until society's opinion began to change during the 1970s when laws were passed in the U.S.A., which made the process legal and allowed husbands to be treated as the legal father of the child. Twenty years later the U.K. also made donor insemination legal.

*

Cartographers (also known as mapmakers) often place a small piece of incorrect information in their work to prevent illegal reproductions. This is known as a *copyright trap* and may even be as simple as adding their initials in the corner of a city park.

Copyright traps are also found in dictionaries – the most famous is the word *zzxjoanw,* which is defined as a Maori word to mean *drum, fife,* or *conclusion.* It first appeared in a dictionary containing 250 words for various musical instruments and phrases. However, the word has taken on a life of its own and has appeared in several novels.

Lillian Virginia Mountweazel (1942 to 1973) was a photographer and author. She became famous for her portraits of the Sierra Miwok and for her collection of rural American mailbox photographs. Although it was reported in 1973 that Mountweazel had been tragically killed in an explosion it was later revealed that she had been a fictitious character created to protect the contents of the 1975 "New Columbia Encyclopaedia". The word *mountweazel* has taken on a life of its own and is used to describe a copyright trap.

*

In the classic movie "The Wizard of Oz", Dorothy asked what kind of colour-changing horse it was that pulled her and her friends along in a carriage. She was told that it was the *horse of a different colour* and the only one of its kind.

To make the horse a different colour in each scene, it was planned to use various substances to coat the horse. However, as a result of protests by animal rights activists, it was agreed that food colouring would be used. However, that idea had to be scrapped as not only did the horse keep licking the product off but the colours did not appear as vibrant on camera as producers had hoped for. In the end, a paste of Jell-O powder was used.

*

A duffle coat is made from duffel, a thick, coarse woollen material which originated in Duffel - a town in the province of Antwerp in Belgium. The design of the coat initially came from the Polish military frock coat.

One of the most famous duffel coat wearers is Paddington Bear. When Paddington arrived in England as a stowaway from darkest Peru, he was only wearing a bush hat that belonged to his Uncle Pastuzo. The duffle coat was given to him by the Browns shortly after they took him home from Paddington Station.

On the 13th of October 2008, Google dedicated a doodle to Paddington to celebrate his 50th birthday.

*

A *purlicue* is the distance between your pointer finger and thumb when extended.

Mel Blanc (1908 to 1989) was an American actor who was known as *The Man of 1,000 Voices*. One voice in particular that he was famous for was that of Bugs Bunny which he did for more than fifty years.

For authenticity, Blanc would chew on a real carrot when performing the voice and then spit it out. This created urban myths such as, he was allergic to carrots, or that he despised the taste. Neither was correct – the fact was that he just wasn't fond of the taste but as a true professional chewed on them for the scene.

In 1961 Blanc was involved in a near-fatal car accident that left him in a coma for weeks. During this time one of the neurologists tried a different approach to get a response and asked Blanc how Bugs Bunny was doing today to which Blanc replied in the voice of Bugs Bunny "just fine doc – how are you?" The doctor reported that it was like Bugs Bunny was trying to save his life.

Bugs Bunny first appeared in a 1938 cartoon for Porky Pig although at that time he did not have a name.

Located a few miles from Knoxville, Tennessee is the "University of Tennessee Anthropological Research Facility" which is nicknamed as the *body farm*. The 2.5-acre plot appears as a serial killer's dumping ground as corpses are left strewn across the woodland. At any time, there are between 150 and 190 human cadavers strategically positioned in a range of scenarios to simulate various crime scenes. There are clothed bodies, naked bodies, bodies in cars, and bodies underneath the water, all situated in different yet potentially real-life circumstances which supply researchers with a better understanding of the decomposition process.

When the centre opened in 1981 it had just one; today it possesses over 700 hundred cadavers, which is one of the largest collections of modern skeletal remains in the world.

*

 Zero degrees Celsius is 32 degrees Fahrenheit.

-40°C and -40°F are identical as that is the point at which both temperature scales converge.

*

Eugène Vidocq (1775 to 1857) a French soldier, criminal, and privateer opened the first known private detective agency in 1833. It was called "Le Bureau des Renseignements" and was staffed by ex-convicts. The official law enforcement tried many times to put him out of business and had Vidocq arrested on suspicious of unlawful imprisonment and taking money under false pretences. Although he was sentenced to five years' imprisonment, the Court of Appeals released him; Vidocq suspected that he had been set-up.

Today, Vidocq is acknowledged for the introduction of detailed record-keeping, criminology, and ballistics, to criminal investigations. He is also credited for creating indelible ink, unalterable bond paper, and for making the first plaster-cast of shoe impressions.

Vidocq is regarded as the first private detective. When Vidocq gave his allegiance to the police force, he persuaded his superiors to allow his agents to wear plain clothes or disguises depending on the situation. His interrogation method was also different in that he invited those he arrested to have dinner with him during which time he often obtained confessions, recruited future informants, and even employed new agents.

*

The dots on dice and dominoes are called *pips*.

*

The acronym Yahoo! stands for *yet another hierarchical officious oracle!* - a phrase coined by two electrical engineering PhD candidates, David Filo and Jerry Yang. The pair decided that *hierarchical* described how the Yahoo! database was arranged in directory layers; *officious* depicted how many office workers would use the database while surfing the internet at work, while *oracle* was intended to mean the source of truth and wisdom.

*

There are approximately 7.71 billion people in the world (February 2019), which is expected to grow to eight billion within the next five years or so.

China has the largest population with 1.419 billion.

The least populated is the independent sovereign entity known as The Holy See (which is often referred to as the Vatican and defined as a country in its own right) which has a population of just 799.

*

The Duke of Edinburgh, Prince Philip, was born in Greece shortly before his family were exiled. Born into Greek and Danish royal families, he was a member of the House of Schleswig-Holstein-Sonderburg-Glücksburg.

Before his official engagement to Princess Elizabeth, he abandoned his Greek and Danish royal titles and became a naturalised British subject; he adopted the surname "Mountbatten" from his maternal grandparents.

Before 1917, members of the British Royal family did not have a surname but were known by the names of the countries they ruled. King George V changed the tradition and adopted the surname Windsor and in doing so declared that all descendants in the male line of Queen Victoria would bear the Windsor name. In 1960, this rule was altered by the Queen and the Duke of Edinburgh when they decided that they would like their direct descendants to be distinguished from the rest of the royal family. It was declared in the Privy Council that their descendants, apart from those with the style of Royal Highness and the title of Prince/Princess, or females who married, would carry the Mountbatten-Windsor name.

*

If a doctor says that (s)he is going to perform *auscultation*, they mean that they will listen to the internal sounds of the body by using a stethoscope.

*

Over two years, Saddam Hussein donated three pints of blood, which, when mixed with chemicals, was used by skilled artists to write a copy of the Koran.

*

"YouTube" was created in February 2005 by Chad Hurley, Steve Chen, and Jawed Karim. The idea was allegedly inspired following Janet Jackson's famous wardrobe malfunction at the Superbowl in 2004, and the Indian Ocean tsunami the same year. Karim searched online to find footage of both events, and upon discovering that it was not that easy to find any, he came up with the innovative idea of creating a video-sharing site.

The first video uploaded was that of Karim discussing the size of elephants' trunks during a visit to the zoo.

Google bought YouTube in 2006 for £883 m ($1.65 bn).

*

Josephine Cochrane (1839 to 1913) (the grand-daughter of John Fitch who invented the steamboat) is accredited with inventing the dishwasher.

Born into a wealthy family with a background in engineering, Cochrane was exposed to a busy social life and entertainment at the family mansion. When she grew up, she became annoyed that the servants kept chipping the expensive fine china, so she decided that it was best to do the washing up herself. One morning, while washing dishes from a social gathering the night before, Cochrane had an epiphany and decided to invent a machine that would actually clean the dishes for her. Four years later, in 1886, she started to advertise her newly formed company ("Garis-Cochran Dish-washing Machine company") and its dishwashing machine. Her big break came a few years later when in 1893 a well-known company (which was continually experiencing growth) used her equipment in its large kitchens. Today Cochrane's company is part of the Whirlpool Corporation.

Even though Cochrane was successful, she was not actually the first person to come up with the idea of a machine that would wash dishes. The first documented evidence of a dishwasher dates back to 1850 when a patent was given to Joel Houghton.

*

A *grawlix* is a sequence of typographical symbols, such as @#*%$, which are used to represent an offensive word or phrase.

*

A *minced oath* is a euphemism created by misspelling or mispronouncing an offensive or profane word, such as fudge, darn, and shoot.

*

"Apple" was founded by Steve Jobs, Steve Wozniak, and Ronald Wayne in April 1976 with shares divided 45%, 45% and 10% respectively.

Even though the first business deal was with a company that had the reputation of not settling their debts, Jobs and Wozniak borrowed $15,000 to ensure they could fulfil the order. At that time, Wayne was the only one who was a homeowner and was conscious that if the deal went sour, he would be the one to suffer a loss as his partners did not have any assets and very little cash. So, just twelve days after the company was set up, Wayne had his name legally removed and sold his shares to Wozniak for $800. Wayne also had concerns that if he remained part of the company, he would just become an administrator who would shuffle papers about all day and not get to be involved in any of the exciting projects.

During an interview held many years later, Wayne stated that while he had never been rich, he had never wanted for anything either and not once did he regret his decision.

*

Every airport in the word has a 3-letter code that is maintained by the "International Air Transport Association" (IATA). These codes are generally used for airline timetables, reservations, and luggage tags.

Airport codes were traditionally determined by radio transmitters, weather stations, cities, or in some instances the name of the original fields in which they were located. For those that historically just used two letters to represent the airport, they simply added an "x" to keep in line with regulations (e.g. Los Angeles changed from LA to LAX).

The "International Civil Aviation Organisation" (ICAO), which is a specialised agency of the United Nations that codifies the principles and procedures of international air navigation, has another coding system which is a four-character code used to identify different aviation facilities such as weather stations, international flight service stations, and area control centres. The ICAO code is not used to the same extent by the airlines as the IATA coding.

There are currently 17,678 airports in the world which are categorised as commercial, i.e. they receive airliners, cargo, and business aircraft. However, if all airports, aerodromes, and airfields were taken into the equation for both civilian and military, the figure would rise to 41,788.

*

The original artwork produced for Disney's "Snow White and the Seven Dwarfs" contained another sixteen dwarfs that did not make it into the final production. While political correctness was far from the public's mind during the late 1930s, the dwarfs who were abandoned were called: - Baldy, Burpy, Deafy, Dizzy, Gabby, Hickey, Jumpy, Lazy, Nifty, Puff, Shorty, Sniffy, Stuffy, Swift, Tubby, and Wheezy.

*

Loch Ness is a freshwater lock in the Scottish Highlands which measures approximately 22.5 miles long by 1.5 miles wide. It is around 755 feet deep and contains more water than all the rivers and lakes in England and Wales combined.

Loch Ness never freezes due to a thermocline effect, i.e. as the water in the highest one-hundred metres cools down it sinks and is replaced by water from the depths which never alters from 6.5°C (44°F).

The first sighting of the Loch Ness Monster (affectionally known as Nessie) was by St. Columba when he went for a swim in 565 A.D.; the first modern-day sighting was on 2nd May 1933.

To date, the most extensive search for the monster took place in 1987; the project, known as Operation Deepscan, was led by Adrian Shrine. No expense was spared, and with researchers using the most advanced sonar and camera technology at that time, the bill soared to £1 million. Regardless that three possible sonar contacts were picked up, the team failed to supply enough evidence to convince the scientific community that the monster existed.

Robert H. Rines (1922 to 2009) from Boston, Massachusetts, dedicated thirty-seven years trying to find the monster which he described as looking like a plesiosaur (a dinosaur which lived underwater). Besides being a lawyer, professor, researcher, and a composer, Dr Rines was also an inventor; he developed the sonar technology that researchers were using when they found the Titanic. Although he held more than eight-hundred patents, he will probably be remembered more for his determined pursuit of "Nessie".

Thomas the Tank Engine first appeared on TV screens during 1984.

Ringo Starr may be the most memorable narrator for the U.K. series as he did the voice-over for seasons 1 and 2 which aired from 1984 to 1986. Other famous people who have narrated are Michael Angelis (series 3 to 16 (1991 to 2012)) and Mark Moraghan (2013 onwards).

In 2014, officials in Portland, Oregon, drained thirty-eight million gallons of drinking water from one of the city's reservoirs after a 19-year-old man was caught urinating into it.

However, due to the expense, which was indirectly passed on to the customers, there was a backlash of complaints saying that the action was unnecessary when the fact that birds and animals die in the reservoir is taken into consideration.

One of the biggest music hits in 1983 was "Every Breath You Take" by "The Police". It was also one of the most misunderstood songs of all time as most people interpreted it as a love song when, in fact, it was a song about stalking. The Police frontman wrote it after separating from his first wife. Described as a nice tune with classic relative-minor chords the words describe how the stalker would be watching every move, every step, every smile, that his prey would take!

Contrary to the initial speculation that gorillas belch when they are happy, a thirty-year study by biologist and conservationist, Ian Redmond, concluded that the noise is actually a contact call. While gorillas can be very loud and dramatic, when it is necessary to be heard through dense vegetation, their contact call is actually part of their etiquette. Redmond learned that the best way to get close to them was to imitate the belch-like sound, fold his arms, and look away, indicating that he was not a threat. Gorillas use this approach to ensure that they do not take others by surprise and to demonstrate that they come in peace.

*

By just using the sense of hearing, it is possible to determine whether hot or cold water is being poured. The reason that there is a different sound is that water is viscous, i.e. it has a thick consistency. A thick liquid resists motion because its molecular makeup gives it a lot of internal friction. However, when water is heated, the viscosity tends to decrease as the temperature rises. When compared to a substance like honey, which will flow much easier when heated, it is difficult to see the difference with water. However, viscosity affects the way that water splashes into a container, so a change in temperature will alter the sound that is made.

*

Carl Panzram was born in Minnesota during 1891 and raised in a poor farming family. His father abandoned him when he was about 8-years-old, and shortly afterwards, Panzram turned to a life of crime. After committing a string of burglaries he was sent to a reform school where he was punished by beatings and rape – as a result, he decided to get even with the world!

To accomplish one of his murder-sprees, he hired ten sailors to work on his yacht. After plying them with alcohol, he shot them all dead.

When he arrived in Lobito Bay, Angola, he hired six local guides to go on a crocodile-hunting expedition. He shot each crew member and fed their corpses to the crocodiles.

He was finally caught and sentenced to imprisonment after admitting to twenty-one murders as well as raping more than 1,000 young boys and men. With brutal honesty, he acknowledged that he was not in the least bit sorry for anything he had done.

During his 25-year sentence, he crushed an employee's head with an iron bar which subsequently got him sent to the gallows in 1930. His last words were "Hurry it up, you Hoosier bastard. I could kill ten men while you're fooling around".

*

While serving a sentence for armed robbery and murder, James Allen (also known as *Red Dog*) (1954 to 1993) was released on parole. During this time, he was placed in a witness protection program so that he could help with investigations into prison gangs.

However, after a night of drinking, he murdered his neighbour by slashing his throat from ear to ear with an incision so deep that the victim was almost decapitated. He then raped and sodomised a woman several times before she escaped. Later that same day he was arrested and subsequently sentenced to death by lethal injection. His last words were an apology to his family whom he told he loved…to the rest of the people he concluded his speech by saying, "you can kiss my ass".

*

George Appel (1886 to 1928) was sentenced to death by

electrocution for murdering a police officer in New York. His final words were "well gentlemen, you are about to see a baked appel".

*

Peter Körten was a German serial killer who drank his victims' blood which immortalised him as the *Vampire of Dusseldorf*. Körten often returned to the scene of the crime and relished in the horror and fear that he had evoked in people. He enjoyed the media attention and would even make contact to give the location of his latest victim.

Körten remained very fond of his wife; with her best interests at heart, he confessed everything to her and suggested that she should turn him in to the police but only on the condition that the authorities pay her a substantial financial reward for doing so.

Without demonstrating any remorse, Körten confessed to seventy-nine acts of crime for which he received nine death sentences. His last words before being beheaded were, "Tell me. After my head has been chopped off will I still be able to hear, at least for a moment, the sound of my own blood gushing from the stump of my neck? That would be a pleasure to end all pleasures".

*

During an open-mic night in the city of Bend in Oregon, 19-year-old Kipp Rusty Walker stepped on stage and sang a song called *Sorry for All the Mess*. While performing, he repeatedly plunged a six-inch blade into his chest which the audience mistakenly thought was part of the act and loudly applauded. However, when Walker collapsed in a pool of blood, they realised the reality and called for medical assistance. Walker's wounds were so severe that he died shortly afterwards.

Walker had only been released a few days earlier from a psychiatric unit where he had been under suicide watch.

The community were divided over his suicide – some people felt sympathetic to his plight while others were outraged that the audience of impressionable young people had been subjected to witnessing the event.

*

Slurry is created from a mixture of cow manure and water; it is used as a natural fertiliser to encourage the growth of grass and crops.

The smell released from the slurry is a mixture of gases which includes methane, carbon dioxide, ammonia, and hydrogen sulphide. The chemicals are produced by bacteria during the decomposition process.

The deadliest gas released is hydrogen sulphide as it affects the nervous system. At low concentrations, the smell can be compared to rotten eggs, but in high levels it is odourless. Each time slurry is mixed, the gases rise, which can be as dangerous outside as it is in confined spaces.

- When slurry smells like rotten eggs the PPM (parts per million) is calculated at 3 to 5.

- At 100-150 ppm, there is the loss of smell.

- 500-700 ppm can cause a person to collapse within five minutes.

- The onset of rapid unconsciousness can occur where there is 700-1,000 ppm; it just takes one or two breaths.

- 1,000-2,000 ppm causes nearly instant death.

Some farmers use anaerobic digesters to convert cow manure into energy. The digester breaks down the manure producing biogas which in turn produces electricity which can be fed into the national grid.

*

During the years of Japan's imperial wars (1931 to 1945), thousands of girls and women were forced to become sex slaves for Japanese troops. Lured with false promises of good jobs, the women (known as *comfort women*) were taken to military bases where they were locked in rooms that measured only 3 feet by 5 feet and were often raped by as many as sixty to seventy soldiers each day.

Seventy years later, in December 2015, Toyoko struck a deal with Seoul claiming that they had found a final and irreversible resolution over the comfort women issue. Prime Minister Shinzo Abe made an apology to those who had suffered, and Japan donated 1 billion yen (£7.18m/$8.99m) to a South Korean fund to help former victims. However, the deal caused a lot of controversies as it did not contain an acknowledgement of legal responsibility by the Japanese government, nor did it provide direct compensation to individual victims.

*

Apparently, spraying antiperspirant on before going to bed at night gives the best possible result the following day.

The job of an antiperspirant is to temporarily plug sweat ducts. As these sweat glands are not as active during the night, there is a better chance of blocking them.

The worst time to apply is when someone is already sweating, e.g. after a shower, as the plugs are not able to form as well in the sweat ducts.

*

The Japanese company, "Thanko", has created a small fan that clips on to the shirt sleeve to circulate air around the armpits. The two batteries can supply up to nine hours blow-drying time; further time can be extended by powering the fans through a USB charger!

*

Cotard's Delusions (also known as Walking Corpse Syndrome) is a rare mental illness with the majority of sufferers believing that they are actually dead. It has been linked to bipolar disorder, depression, and/or schizophrenia.

Another symptom is that the person thinks that they do not exist. However, they realise that they are present somewhere and believe they are incapable of dying. The underlying cause of the condition is not understood, causing the disorder to basically remain a mystery. Some believe that it is not a single disease but rather a condition that is often associated with a combination of other medical conditions such as encephalitis (inflammation of the brain), Parkinson's Disease, or a brain tumour.

Although the first case of Cotard's was recorded in 1788, it was only formally identified in 1880 by French neurologist, Jules Cotard. When an elderly woman was preparing a meal, she felt a cold draft and became temporarily paralysed down one side of her body. Once the paralysis passed and she could speak again, she constantly demanded that her daughters were to wrap her in a shroud and place her in a coffin. They eventually gave it to her demands and laid her out so that she could be mourned. However, during her "wake" she continued complaining about her shroud and moaned that it was not the right colour. The delusions were treated with a mixture containing opium which kept symptoms at bay for a few months at a time.

In 2009, Belgian psychiatrists reported the case of an 88-year-old man who explained to them that he had died and was concerned that he had not been buried yet.

As recently as 2015, a 17-year-old schoolgirl named Haley Smith was reported to be sitting in a classroom when a weird sensation came over her, and she believed that she was dead. She felt compelled to visit graveyards and to watch zombie movies as it made her feel relaxed. After two years she was strong enough to admit the problem to her father and was urged to see a psychiatrist. Watching Disney movies had a significant impact on her recovery as they made her feel good; she questioned how a dead person would be able to experience such a positive emotion.

It is theorised that the distorted reality is caused by a malfunction in the area of the brain called the fusiform gyrus as well as in the amygdala. Treatments include anti-depressants, antipsychotics, as well as the controversial electroconvulsive therapy.

*

There is no mention of Adam and Eve eating an apple in the Bible – the type of fruit they ate is only recorded as being forbidden.

*

A *portmanteau* is a linguistic blend of words, i.e. a word

formed from parts of two or more other words, e.g. *brunch*, which is taken from *breakfast* and *lunch*.

*

QE ii is Queen Elizabeth II.

QE2 was the flagship of the Cunard Line which took its maiden voyage in 1969. It was one of the last great Transatlantic liners and was one of the fastest and grandest passenger vessels ever built.

After forty years, the QE2 had a total sailing time that was equivalent to twenty years of non-stop motion – the ship had circumnavigated the globe twenty-five times.

The QE2 was named after the wife of King George VI, not Queen Elizabeth II, which explains why the actual number is used rather than roman numerals.

*

The RMS Queen Elizabeth was launched in 1938 in honour of Queen Elizabeth (1900 to 2002), who was then the Queen Consort to King George VI. In 1968, the vessel was sold to a group of American businessmen before being sold at auction to an entrepreneur in Hong Kong. However, during a refurbishment, the ship caught fire and the weight of water sprayed on to it by fireboats caused the burnt wreck to capsize and sink in Hong Kong's Victoria Harbour. It was eventually dismantled for scrap.

*

The only T.V. commercial that Elvis Presley actually did was in 1954 for his favourite doughnut shop – "Southern Maid Donuts".

*

A Parisian stray cat was the first and only cat that has been sent into space. Named Félicette, the cat jetted 130 miles above Earth on the 24th October 1963. After soaring high above the Algerian Sahara Desert, she returned to earth via parachute fifteen minutes later. Researchers were eager to study her brain waves to establish if the trip had made any changes. Félicette was decorated as a heroine for her valuable contribution to research.

*

The first T.V. remote control was developed in 1950 by Zenith and was known as the *Lazy Bones*. A motor in the TV set operated a turner through the remote control which was connected via a cable. Although the majority liked the idea of the modern invention, there were complaints about accidents happening as people kept tripping over the unsightly wire strewn across the floor.

*

Noiva do Cordeiro nestles deep within the hills of South-East Brazil, three-hundred miles from Rio de Janeiro. The town is populated and governed almost entirely by six-hundred women of which three-hundred are of working age.

The settlement dates back to 1891 when a local girl was forced to marry a man she didn't love. When she decided to leave her husband, she was excommunicated by the Catholic Church - the ruling also banished the next five generations of her family.

The town's inhabitants are renowned for their beauty as much as they are for their stubbornness at refusing to live in a man's world. There are a few men who live in the town, but that usually is only at weekends.

Apparently, all the women get along with each other and claim that they live in peace and harmony.

*

Sailfish are saltwater fish that reside in warm and temperate ocean waters. Indo-Pacific sailfish can reach eleven feet in length and weigh more than 220 pounds while Atlantic sailfish are on average around six feet long and weigh 128 pounds. Clocked at a speed of 68 mph they are the fastest swimming fish.

*

Lepidopterophobia is the fear of butterflies.

*

In 2012, Benedict Cumberbatch was kidnapped by armed car-jackers in South Africa. After being dragged into the boot of the car, he told his captors that he had a problem with his heart and that he would probably have a fit and die. He was eventually pulled out of the boot and left tied up with his friends. No explanation nor reason was ever given for the ordeal.

*

When someone is given the exact same name as their father who is still alive, they tend to use generation designations such as *Sr* or *Jr.*, e.g. Martin Luther King, Jr., and Robert Downey Jr. If the nominal suffix is II, it would indicate that the first person to bear the name was not the namesake's father – the II most likely honours a grandfather or other male relative.

Natural water is oxygenated to some extent, which means that when water freezes, the impurities such as oxygen and other dissolved gasses, are pushed away from the area most exposed to the extreme temperature. This results in the last part of water to freeze having the most impurities present in it.

When making ice cubes the last part to freeze is at the bottom of the ice-cube as the water freezes from the top downwards – the end result is that the bottom of the ice cube looks like it has milky coloured bits as it was the last place that the impurities had to go.

To make clear ice cubes, the water should be boiled beforehand as oxygen solubility in water decreases when the temperature rises.

*

"Ditto" as a response means the *same here*. It is derived from a dialect variation of the Italian *detto* which translates as *said* or *to say*. It was first recorded to be used in English during the 17th century in a bid to avoid repeating words in accounting and commercial language. Ditto gradually altered from a noun to an adverb to convey that one person agreed with what another has just said.

*

In 1967, the world's first UFO landing pad was built in St. Paul, Canada. In 1990, the town's mayor officially opened a UFO tourist information centre which exhibits photographs of UFO's, crop circles, and cattle mutilations.

*

Typing into Google "do a barrel roll" makes the browser do a barrel roll.

*

Between 1932 and 1972, the U.S. government denied hundreds of African-American men treatment for syphilis as part of a racist medical experiment that was initially only planned to last six months. Known as the "Tuskegee Syphilis Study," it is infamous for being one of the most prolonged and knowingly unethical medical experiments in history.

Researchers observed the untreated men to ascertain whether the disease affected black men differently than white men. They were given placebos, and the truth of their condition was withheld. By the time journalists exposed the experiment only seventy-four of the original participants were still alive; over one-hundred had succumbed to the disease. By that stage, some wives had contracted the disease, and children had been born with congenital syphilis.

In exchange for taking part in the project, the men received free medical exams, free meals, and burial insurance. Although Penicillin had become the drug of choice for treating syphilis in 1947, it was not offered to the participants.

*

Gregory Goodwin Pincus (1903 to 1967) was an American endocrinologist whose work on the antifertility properties of steroids led to the development of the first effective birth-control pill.

In 1934, Pincus successfully created a test-tube rabbit; this breakthrough in artificial insemination caused different opinions as some were excited, while others referred to him as Frankenstein.

By the 1950s, Pincus had developed the "Pill" which was a combination of the hormones oestrogen and progestin. The trials were the most extensive series of clinical tests ever performed - the participants were mostly Puerto Rican women of colour. The government officials supported birth-control as a form of population cleansing in the hope that it would curtail the widespread poverty - in fact, in 1937 it was legally sanctioned that Puerto Rican women could be sterilised for such reasons. These vulnerable women were neither told that the pill was only in its experimental stages nor were they informed of any potentially dangerous side effects.

Following a year of trials, the pill was deemed to be effective at preventing pregnancy regardless that 17% of the test subjects had suffered debilitating side effects such as headaches, vomiting, and stomach pains. Three women had died during the trials, but their cause of death was never investigated.

After the Puerto Rican women had been forced to participate in the trial, the pill was marketed predominately at white women as a symbol of independence. Its dark history was put aside, and within five years of being released, six-million American women were taking it.

It was introduced to the U.K. on the National Health Service in 1961, but until 1967 it was only available for married women.

*

Polyorchidism (also known as supernumerary testes) is a very rare condition which describes the presence of more than two testicles. The extra testicle is usually located in the left sac of the scrotum. Scientific literature indicates that there have been approximately two hundred cases reported.

There are two main types of polyorchidism: -

- *Type A polyorchidism* refers to when the supernumerary testicle is drained by a separate vas deferens and therefore has the potential for reproduction.

- *Type B* refers to the case when the supernumerary testicle is not drained via vas deferens and therefore has no reproductive potential. Most often men with polyorchidism will have three testicles, but the record stands at five.

*

Wilson Greatbatch (1919 to 2011) was an American engineer and revolutionary inventor who held more than 325 patents. Although his inventions largely shaped modern cardiology, he is probably best remembered for creating the implantable pacemaker.

While Greatbatch was working on a device to record the rhythm of heartbeats, he accidentally inserted the wrong circuit component when meant that when the device was activated, it emitted a rhythm instead of recording it. He realised immediately that he had stumbled on a way that would electrically simulate and stimulate a heartbeat.

Over the next few years, he improved and miniaturised the pacemaker and successfully implanted it into a dog in 1958. Two years later, the first human to receive a pacemaker was a 77-year-old man who went on to live for another eighteen months.

In 1988, Greatbatch was inducted into the "National Investors Hall of Fame" in Ohio.

*

When a pregnant woman suffers organ damage, such as that which occurs during a heart attack, the fetus will share stem cells to the damaged organ to help repair it. This transfer and incorporation of fetal stem cells into the mother's organs is known as *fetomaternal microchimerism*.

*

In 1990, Daniel, who later became known as the *Andes Goat Boy*, was found living with a herd of wild goats in the Andes, Peru. For eight years, Daniel had been living in the wild alongside his adopted goat family with whom he was able to communicate. To survive, his diet had consisted of goat's milk, roots, and berries. His feral characteristics, such as walking on all four limbs, had caused his hands and feet to harden due to scar formation.

When Daniel was found, he was not able to communicate in any human language.

*

Borborygmus is the rumbling sound caused by the movement of gas in the digestive system.

As the food is propelled along the system, waves of muscle contractions move and push the contents continually downward in a process called peristalsis. These contractions also help blend the food, liquid, and various digestive juices together into a mixture known as chyme. Accompanying the chyme on its travels are pockets of gases and air which can occasionally get squeezed, causing rumbling noises to occur. These noises can be produced at any time, but they will be much quieter when there is food in the stomach.

One way to minimise the rumbling effect of the process is to eat small meals regularly instead of a few large ones throughout the day. However, it is not always possible to eat something when the rumbling starts, but one way to reduce the noise is to inhale as much air as possible, hold the breath for as long as possible, and release. This inflates the lungs to their full capacity causing them to push down on the stomach which temporarily compresses it, which in turn reduces movement of the contents and gases.

Approximately two hours after the stomach has emptied itself, it begins to create hormones that stimulate nerves to send information to the brain, which replies by signalling for the digestive muscles to restart the process of peristalsis. The vibrations on an empty stomach can make the person feel hungry.

*

Most bony fish (the group of fish that have skeletons primarily composed of bone tissue as opposed to cartilage) have an internal air-filled organ, known as a *swim bladder*, which contributes to their ability to control buoyancy. The manipulation of the amount of air stored in the swim bladder enables the fish to either go closer to the surface, dive lower, or to stay suspended at a precise depth.

Swim bladders do however have a side effect of making the fish unstable at times, especially if they become ill or are injured. When they lose the ability to maintain balance, the more buoyant part of their body will surface. When fish die, all ability to stop themselves from rolling has gone, which explains why fish float on their sides or upside down when they die.

*

At the age of 16, Michael Lotito (1950 to 2007) ate glass by accident without any issues. From that point-in-time, Lotito consumed nine tonnes of metal which included eighteen bicycles, fifteen supermarket trolleys, seven televisions, six chandeliers, two beds, a pair of skies, a coffin, and an entire Cessna 150 aeroplane.

He suffered from Pica, a medical condition which causes the sufferer to crave non-nutritive things such as dirt, glass, metal, paper, and stone, to name a few! Fortunately for Lotito, his stomach and intestines had a thick lining which made it possible for sharp objects to pass through his system without causing any damage.

He was nicknamed *Monsieur Mangetout* (Mr Eat-All) and provided the only example in history of a coffin ending up inside a man.

His doctors took blood samples and scanned his internal organs, which revealed that there had not been any unusual effects on his body due to his strange eating habits.

Lotito did have trouble eating and digesting bananas and hard-boiled eggs!

*

Glancing at something, or someone requires a categorisation process to occur while recognition checks take place. However, if there is a small deviation in what is expected, e.g. a scar or a large birthmark, the brain is sent into overdrive causing the scan for recognition to take longer than usual or to even turn into a stare. Although staring is considered rude, a study in 2012 at the "University of Southern California" concluded that when participants were watching an able-bodied person carrying out a specific task the participant's brain activity was rather quiet. However, when the participants observed someone with a disability doing the exact same thing the participant's brains showed enormous levels of activeness at the start but as they continued watching the brain activity lessened to the same level as when watching the first group of able-bodied subjects. This research would imply that by looking at something or someone who is deemed different for a more prolonged period can help us to develop knowledge about the situation and engage empathy.

*

Barack Obama first made history, and the national headlines, when he was elected as the first black president of the Harvard Law Review in the spring of 1990.

*

999 is the world's oldest emergency call service which was put into place in London, England, on the 1st July 1937.

It was initiated after a fire in 1935 claimed the lives of five women. Witnesses of the disaster had been unable to get through to the operator for help as the switchboard was busy. In light of this, it was suggested that a three-digit number should be used as it would be easier to dial from a dark or smoke-filled environment. The number 111 was rejected as it could be triggered by faulty equipment; the first telephone numbers represented the first three letters of a particular company, so 999 was agreed as the most sensible choice.

The U.S.A. did not have a standard emergency number before 1968. When the Federal Communications Commission met with AT&T to establish an emergency number, they selected 911 as it had never been designated for an office code, area code, or service code.

A 911 call that went viral in 2015 was made by a 5-year-old

girl named Savannah who took over the emergency call as her father was having great difficulty breathing. With instructions from the dispatch, she unlocked the front door to enable medics to enter. Meanwhile, she voluntarily encouraged her father and told him not to worry. However, when she realised that the paramedics would see her in her pyjamas, she thought it best to get dressed but admitted her dilemma to the call handler as she was not sure what to wear!

*

Daniel Edgar Sickles (1819 – 1914), who was born into a wealthy family in New York City, had a career as a politician, soldier, and diplomat.

Despite the objections of his family, Sickles married Teresa Bagioli, who at the age of 15 years old was eighteen years his junior. Notorious for being a lady's man, he left his pregnant wife at home while he went on a business trip accompanied by a prostitute named Fanny White.

Regardless that Sickles had numerous extramarital affairs, he was absolutely outraged when he discovered that his neglected wife was having a relationship with the District Attorney of Columbia, Philip Barton Key II. Sickles demanded his wife to make a written confession and then proceeded to shot Key in the groin, thigh, and chest.

Sickles admitted to the murder and was held in custody awaiting his trial. However, instead of being treated as a criminal, he was visited by so many influential visitors that he was given the use of the head prison wardens apartment to meet and greet his guests.

Sickles' lawyer argued that his client was so distraught upon learning of his wife's unfaithfulness that he was temporarily driven insane. The newspapers supported this argument, which was fuelled further when the wife's written confession was leaked. The jury believed the defence plea and Sickles was released without penalty; in fact, he was seen as the hero as by killing his wife's lover he had done the women in society a favour by protecting them from the evil lustfulness of a sexual predator.

This was the first legal case of temporary insanity and set a new legal precedent.

When Sickles publicly forgave, and reconciled with his wife, the public and his supporters were apparently more outraged than by the murder and unorthodox acquittal.

*

During its economic peak, the coal mining town of Centralia, Pennsylvania, had around one-thousand inhabitants; at the last count, the population had reduced to nine.

In 1963, five volunteers were cleaning up the landfill which was located in an abandoned mine pit. After setting the rubbish on fire, they let all the contents burn to ash and then extinguished it – or so they thought. It is believed that the fire spread through a hole in the rock pit into an underground coal mine where it grew in intensity and has continued to burn for the last forty-four years. The underground fire covers approximately five-hundred acres.

Coal seam fires are not that uncommon – scientists claim that there are apparently thousands of them burning underground at the present time. It is estimated that 2-3% of the world's industrial carbon emissions may come from uncontained coal fires in China alone where it is said that fires burn up to twenty million tons of coal each year.

The oldest burning coal seam is Mount Wingen in New South Wales. As it burns it slowly moves south along the mountain at a rate of one meter per year. In its history, the seam has covered a total of 4 miles (6.5 km) suggesting that it has been smouldering for 6,000 years. It was initially thought that volcanic activity was the cause of the fire, but researchers have established that it was most likely either started by a lightning strike or a bush fire.

*

The first known flight attendant was Heinrich Kubis who began working on the passenger airship *LZ 10 Schwaben* in March 1912; the LZ 10 Schwaben is regarded as the first commercially successful passenger-carrying aircraft.

Kubis was onboard the infamous *LZ 129 Hindenburg* when the airship dining room burst into flames at Lakehurst, New Jersey, on 6th May 1937. When the Hindenburg sank close enough to the ground, Kubis, along with passengers and other crew members, jumped from the windows. Although Kubis was unhurt thirty-five of the ninety-seven passengers were killed. The disaster had a massive impact on the public's confidence in airships and brought the airship era to an abrupt end.

Although the Hindenburg's tragic end made it the most famous airship disaster, it was not the worst accident. In 1933, a U.S. Navy airship had only three survivors from a total of seventy-six passengers.

*

After a long battle against sexism, Ellen Church (1904 - 1965) became the first female flight attendant.

As a licensed pilot and a registered nurse, Church knew the

airlines would not be interested in hiring female pilots in the 1930s. She appealed to the airline executives and recommended that nurses be hired to perform some of the tasks carried out by the co-pilots – tasks such as hauling luggage, cleaning the cabin, helping to refuel, bolting down seats before take-off, and handing out food and drinks. The executives of Boeing Air Transport went for her pitch, recognising that having a nurse onboard would be psychologically beneficial for passengers.

On the 15th May 1930 Church, along with seven other women, took their first flight. Once the benefits of having female flight attendants were clearly seen, more female flight attendants were recruited throughout the industry. However, the application process remained steeped in sexism as applicants had to be pretty, petite, single, graduate nurses, aged between 21 to 26 years old, and weigh between 100 to 120 lbs.

*

The American restaurant, the "Heart Attack Grill" has been fighting anorexia since it first opened its doors in 2005. The restaurant has a hospital-based theme with waitresses scantily dressed in nurses' uniforms and customers supplied with hospital gowns.

Choices on the menu include single, double, triple, and quadruple bypass hamburgers, which can be ordered with a side dish of flat-liner fries which are cooked in pure lard. Wine is delivered on a hospital-style drip.

Anyone who weighs over 300 lbs gets to eat for free.

Those that finish the biggest burger are given a free wheelchair ride out to their car; for those that do not eat all that they ordered their personal nurse/waitress spanks them in front of all the other diners.

According to the owner, the octuple bypass burger contains 19,900 calories, which is almost the number of calories the average person would consume over 10 days.

Customers have been taken away from the restaurant in ambulances after having heart attacks. One person actually died in the restaurant.

Blair River, the 29-year-old spokesman for the restaurant, got to eat for free every time he visited as he weighed 570 lbs. He died in March 2011 following complications from pneumonia. During an interview, the restaurant's owner, Jon Basso, produced the cremated ashes of another spokesman and placing them on a table said that his message to people is that this is what happens if people do not analyse their eating habits – food for thought! Critics suggest that he is actually marketing to those that have enormous resentment about being told to eat a healthy diet.

*

When it was recommended that George Washington's portrait should be printed on American currency, the president objected. This set an unwritten precedent which eventually became law that no living person can appear on U.S. coinage - presidents must be dead for at least two years before they are eligible for inclusion in the Presidential Dollar series.

This prohibition only applies to coins in circulation -living presidents can have their image featured on commemorative coins.

*

In May 2016, the obituary of Mary Anne Noland from Virginia

stated that *faced with the prospect of voting for either Donald Trump or Hilary Clinton she decided to die instead.*

Her husband told the press that one of her sons wrote the obituary in a light-hearted way, not as a political statement but rather to capture and honour his mother's sense of humour.

*

On the 1st April 2015, Burger King in Japan launched a burger-scented cologne. The scent was named "Flame-Grilled" and supposedly imitated the aroma of the Whopper Burger which consists of flame-grilled beef, onions, lettuce, and mayonnaise.

Before the launch, many speculated that it was an April Fool's Day joke. When it was released, it was described as the scent of seduction with a hint of flame-broiled meat.

*

When the marriage of Albert Einstein to his first wife and mother of his children, Mileva Marić, became strained he set out a list of conditions that she had to agree to if she wanted him to return to their home. The demands were such things as being supplied with three main meals regularly in his room, that all personal relations would cease to exist unless necessary for social occasions, that she should not expect intimacy from him, that she would stop talking to him if he requested it, and that she would not belittle him in front of their children.

Due to the relationship deteriorating beyond repair the couple agreed to divorce in 1919 after having lived apart for five years. As a financial agreement, Einstein proposed that Mileva could receive the money that he would one day hopefully receive for winning a Nobel Prize. Pondering the condition for a week, Mileva accepted the offer which paid off in 1921 when Einstein won the Nobel Prize in Physics.

In 1919 Einstein married Elsa Löwenthal whom he had been involved with since 1912. She was his first cousin maternally and a second cousin, paternally.

*

The largest employer in the world is the U.S. Department of Defence, which has a workforce of around 3.2 million.

The largest non-government employer is Walmart, which has an estimated 2.1 million employees.

*

Rothschild is a name that has been associated with international banking since the late 1700s. Ranked as the wealthiest family in the world, they are renowned for being very private and keeping a low profile. Likewise, their business activities are also kept private, so it is difficult to estimate their wealth, but it is speculated to be at least $350 billion (although, in theory, it could possibly range into trillions).

The original patriarch, Mayer Rothschild, was a favoured assistant and finance manager of the German royal family. He used his position to develop a banking business for German aristocracy, and his five sons eventually were stationed across Europe to manage local banking affairs.

Many conspiracy theorists believe that the Rothschilds have handpicked presidents, orchestrated wars, bankrupted countries, and even caused market crashes to gain more global wealth. It is said that Nathan Rothschild heard before anyone else that the Battle of Waterloo was not a lost cause; with that knowledge, Nathan went to the London Stock Exchange and sold all of his bonds in the British government. This caused panic as the public believed losing the battle would financially devastate the country. Stock prices fell drastically as everyone rushed to sell off their own shares, but when the prices were at an all-time low, Nathan hoovered up all the shares making him primarily the owner of all of England's finances.

It is rumoured that many of the family members are believed to be Satanists; visitors to their home have claimed that there was a place at the table where no one could sit as it was reserved for Satan.

*

On the 26th January 1972, 22-year-old flight attendant Vesna Vulović was working on a JAT flight 367 when the plane exploded and split apart. According to investigators, Vulović was trapped by a food trolley in the plane's tail section as it plummeted to earth where it landed in a densely wooded and snow-blanketed part of the mountainside. When Vulović was found, she had a fractured skull, two crushed vertebrae, several broken ribs, broken legs, and a broken pelvis; she was temporarily paralysed from the waist down and was in a coma for ten days.

In time, Vulović made a full recovery and returned to work at a desk job for the airline. She was honoured by Yugoslavia's Communist leader and celebrated as a national hero. She gained a place in the Guinness Book of Records in 1985 for surviving the highest fall (33,000 feet) without a parachute.

She continued to fly as a passenger, which she said was probably due to the lack of memory of the accident.

*

Yuri Gagarin (1934 – 1968) was a Russian Soviet pilot and cosmonaut (the job title for someone that has been selected, completed the training, and been certified by the Russian Space Agency); he was the first person to travel into outer space when his spacecraft completed an orbit of the Earth on the 12th April 1961.

There are many rituals followed through on the day before the launch of a spaceflight. These generally pay homage to the launch-day behaviour of space-flight pioneers.

For Russian cosmonauts, the launch day preparations start two weeks beforehand. They include signing a guest book in Gagarin's old office, planting a tree, getting a haircut, watching the 1969 movie "White Sun of the Desert", and as they leave the hotel room to make their way to the launch pad, they sign their room door.

A relatively new tradition has been added – that of a religious blessing performed by a Russian Orthodox priest just before the crew board a bus for the final stage of the journey. The last tradition to be carried out is for the bus to stop en route and for each member to take their turn urinating over the back-right tyre. Women are excused from taking part in the urination ritual, but if they do wish to participate, they can bring a vial of urine with them to pour on the tyre. It is said that Gagarin was on his way to the launch pad when he needed to urinate one last time!

*

The best place to launch a spacecraft is from the equator. The earth's surface is moving at 1,040 mph (1,670 kph) at the equator whereas land halfway to the pole is only going at 733 mph (1,180 kph). Launching from the equator makes the spacecraft move almost 310 mph (500 kph) faster after it is launched. The greater the speed boost, the less energy required to get into space, which reduces the amount of fuel needed.

*

The collective noun for a group of flamingos is a flamboyance.

*

Snowboarding became an official Winter Olympic sport in the 1998 games held in Nagano, Japan.

The first variation of snowboarding began in the 1960s when an American man, Sherman Poppen, strapped two skies together and added rope to help steer. This type of snow surfing was called *snurfer*.

*

Karaoke translates as an *empty orchestra*.

The idea was born in Japan during 1971 when businessman and musician, Daisuke Inoue, supplied a client with a taped version of musical backup as he was attending an event unaccompanied. As it was a success, Inoue saw potential and began renting out machines that were outfitted with cassette decks and amplifiers.

When Inoue was awarded the Ig Nobel Peace Prize in 2004, his acceptance speech included a karaoke rendition – the address won him the most prolonged standing ovation in the history of the awards.

*

The first ATM (Automated Teller Machine) was put into use on the 27th June 1967 at Barclays Bank, London, England.

Today it is estimated that there are over three million ATMs'
worldwide.

*

The only even prime number (a number which can only be
divided by itself and by 1) is the number 2.

Except for 0 and 1, a number is either a prime or composition
number (a figure defined as greater than 1 which is not a
prime number).

*

The name for the Scandinavian retail chain "Ikea" is an
acronym: -

- the first two letters are the initials of the owner's name -
  Ingvar Kamprad,

- E is for the name of the farm he grew up in - *Elmtaryd,*

- and the A is for a nearby village – *Agunnaryd.*

The world's biggest Ikea is in Stockholm; it covers 594,000
square feet.

*

The "real" name for the Scooby-Doo character "Shaggy" is
Norville Rogers.

Scooby-Doo's real name is Scoobert Doo.

*

Moles have a subterranean lifestyle and spend most of their
time digging tunnels. However, these are more than just a
network of highways as they dig individual chambers that

serve as bedrooms and a kitchen. A mole can dig and push soil at a force of forty times their body weight. To fuel their energy, they eat their body weight in food every day.

Their diet consists mostly of earthworms, and as many as 470 worms have been recorded in one kitchen. To keep their food fresh, the mole immobilises the worms by biting their heads off.

Moles are solitary creatures - apart from breeding times, they remain in their own territory. It is considered unusual if there are more than five moles in any one acre.

Baby moles are known as pups and are ready to leave the nest after five to six weeks.

On average, the lifespan of a mole is three years.

There are not any moles in Ireland nor Northern Ireland. The DIY retailer B&Q made the error by stocking their stores with sonic mole repellers for several months before they realised why they were not selling.

*

Markus Alexej Persson is a Swedish video game programmer and designer who is best known for founding the company Mojang for the principal purpose of releasing Minecraft.

In June 2014 Persson put out a tweet to gauge the interest of any outside parties in purchasing his Mojang shares. Three months later the company was sold to Microsoft for $2.5 billion.

*

"Willy Wonka and the Chocolate Factory" was released in 1971. It is estimated today that Willy Wonka's net worth would be £1.96 billion/$2.3 billion.

*

The sword-billed hummingbird found in the Andes of South America is the only species of bird that has a bill longer than its body which enables it to feed on flowers with long corollas.

When perching, the sword-billed hummingbird must hold its long bill up high in order to balance.

*

The first radio show for entertainment and music was broadcast from Brant Rock, Massachusetts, on Christmas Eve 1906. The presenter was a Canadian born inventor, Reginal A. Fessenden (1866 to 1932), who played a phonograph record of Handel's "Ombra Mai Fu", followed by the Christmas carol "O Holy Night". The show concluded with a reading from the Holy Bible, which gives an account of the birth of the Lord Jesus Christ (Luke chapter 2).

A repeat broadcast performance was given on New Year's Eve.

Fessenden's wife was present at the broadcast but apparently had stage fright which kept her from participating.

*

Bethlem, Pennsylvania, is listed in the Top 100 best places to live.

It was given its name on Christmas Eve 1741 when Christian missionaries arrived and founded the community. While singing "Not Jerusalem, but Lowly Bethlehem" during an evening worship service, they observed the animals and immediately thought that Bethlehem was an apt name for the settlement. Today the city is home to approximately 750,000 people.

"Bethlem Steel Corporation" became a pioneering company during the industrial revolution and was America's second-largest steel producer and largest shipbuilder. Steel from the company was used in the George Washington Bridge, The Chrysler Building, the Rockefeller Centre, the Hoover Dam, the Golden Gate Bridge, Alcatraz prison, and in thousands of ships. The company was in operation for over 150 years before it closed its doors in 2003.

*

Hoover Dam was initially known as Boulder Dam. It took fourteen years before it was officially named due to political disagreements and resentment to President Hoover.

*

The highest mountain in Austria is the *Grossglockner*.

*

Nevada is nicknamed as *the Silver State* due to the silver rush days of the mid-1800s.

California is nicknamed as *the Golden State* following the discovery of gold in 1848. Another reason is due to golden-yellow poppy fields that bring colour during spring.

Nevada and California are the only two states that have precious metals as part of their nicknames.

*

Nevada's state prison had a casino in it from 1932 to 1967.

*

August Fey (who had his name changed to Charles Fey) was the German inventor who created the slot machine. Records vary as to the exact year but the two most commonly quoted are 1887 and 1895.

*

Macau, China, (officially known as the *Macao Special Administration Region of the People's Republic of China*) has its own monetary system, legal system, and immigration policy, which make it distinct from the laws of China. It is the only Chinese territory where it is legal to gamble in a casino – in fact, more money flows through Macau's casinos than anywhere else in the world.

*

A *croupier* is a person appointed at a gambling table to assist in the conduct of the game.

*

Before 2008, George Eyser (1870 to 1919) was the only person with an artificial leg to have competed in the Olympic Games. Having survived being run over by a train, which resulted in his leg being amputated from below the knee, he trained as a gymnast with the American "Concordia Turnverein Gymnastic Team" and competed at the 1904 Summer Olympic Games. He was the third top medallist of the Games and won three golds, two silvers, and one bronze.

*

Britain's oldest skeleton was unearthed in one of the country's most beautiful stalactite caverns, Gough's Cave at Cheddar Gorge in Somerset.

Known as the *Cheddar Man,* the skeleton was found in 1903. It is calculated that the man died some 9,000 years ago.

During the filming of a television series on archaeology, twenty locals, who were historically connected for generations to the area, had their DNA tested. Schoolteacher, Adrian Targett, took part in the testing and it was discovered that the two men had a maternal ancestor. This is the longest, confirmed time that has been traced between relatives. In comparison, the Royal family can only record its heritage back to King Egbert of Wessex who ruled from 802 A.D. to 830 A.D.

*

The shortest commercial flight in the world is from Westray (one of the Orkney Islands in Scotland) to Papa Westray. The distance is 1.7 miles and if the wind is blowing in the pilots favour the Loganair flight can be completed in just 47 seconds. The maximum duration is two minutes.

*

The shortest international flight covers thirteen miles and lasts eight minutes. "People's Viennaline" run the service between St. Gallen-Altenrhein Airport in Switzerland and Friedrichshafen in Germany.

*

The American expression *OK* is used worldwide although its roots actually lie in a joke. On the 23rd March 1839, the editor of the Boston Morning Post published a humorous article about an anti-bell ringing society. At the end of his column was written OK to state that all was correct (at that time it was the trend to abbreviate using different first letters of words, e.g. ok stood for *all korrect*).

During the Presidential election in 1840 supporters for Martin van Buren, who was known by his nickname Old Kinderhook, created the O.K. Club. By the 1870s it was used for various purposes, e.g. telegraph operators had adopted it to acknowledge receiving a transmission, and its use and meaning spread from there.

*

The travelling "National Poo Museum" is the brainchild of Daniel Roberts and is intended to inform visitors about human and animal health along with educating spectators about sewer systems and the use of excrement as an energy source.

Opening its tour at the Isle of Wight's zoo, the display of eighteen samples of encapsulated faeces ranged from that of a human baby to an adult lion. Exhibits were strategically arranged, e.g. a cat's poo was placed in a shoe, and one specimen even had teeth and bones in it. The show is aptly called "Poo at the Zoo".

*

A kidney donation can be from either a living or deceased donor. The new kidney is placed in the lower part of the abdomen, but in most cases, the patient's own kidney is not removed.

The removal of native kidneys is a major operation that can require six to eight weeks for recovery. Dialysis needs to begin immediately once the organ is removed. Some people require blood transfusions either during or after the procedure, but transfusions can result in the development of antibodies that could potentially attack and destroy a transplanted kidney.

Their job is to filter blood - about 45 gallons of blood per day. They also rid the body of waste products as well as regulating blood pressure and making red blood cells.

Each kidney has around 1.5 million blood-filtering units, which are called nephrons. However, only 300,000 nephrons are needed to filter blood properly which is why it is possible to survive with only one healthy kidney.

*

A frog's tongue is attached to and folded up in the front part of its mouth rather than at the back. When extended, it measures about a third the length of a frog – in comparison, this would mean a human's tongue would reach to their belly button!

Examination of various frog species discovered that their tongues were among the softest biological materials ever measured.

Researchers at the Georgia Institute of Technology, Atlanta, discovered that the leopard frog can use its tongue to catch insects in less than 0.07 seconds which is five times faster than a human blink.

Immediately the frog's prey is attached, the tongue retracts which is when sections of fat and muscle act as built-in shock absorbers to dampen the energy released by the impact and in turn stop the insect from falling off despite the significant forces exerted upon it.

Further analysis was conducted to understand what makes a frog's tongue sticky. Studies concluded that their saliva has properties that change depending on the force applied - when the tongue strikes an insect the saliva (which is highly viscous) flows freely and seeps into every area but when it starts to retract the saliva thickens again holding onto the captured meal. However, when the insect is in the frog's mouth, the frog has the challenge of getting it off its tongue. Although it may be challenging to pull the insect off, it is comparably easy to slide it off. The solution – the frog uses its eyeballs by retracting them inwards to push the meal off its tongue.

*

A human's tongue is the only muscle that works without any support from the skeleton – it is known as a *muscular hydrostat*. It is anchored to the mouth by tough tissue and mucosa; at the back of the mouth, the tongue is anchored into the hyoid bone (oropharynx) which is the only bone in the human body not connected to another.

The colour of the tongue can tell a lot about a person's health, which explains why a doctor will ask a patient to stick it out: -

- a pink tongue indicates good health,
- a white coating would suggest a fungal infection,
- yellow denotes a stomach problem or fever.

The average tongue measures 10 cms (4 inches) long when measured from where it begins at the back of the throat (the place that is between the soft palate and the hyoid bone) to the tip. Nick Stoeberl from California, holds the record for the longest tongue – it measures 10.1 cms. Stoeberl found that he was able to use it as a paintbrush – a process he calls *licking*. From all of the portraits and artwork that he has created, he is proudest of *licking* a giant beaver which also earned him a place in the record books.

*

Eyelashes usually measure one-third the length of the person's eyes which scientist have discovered is just the right length to minimise the flow of air over the eyeballs and to stop irritating dust particles from getting deposited on the surface.

To ensure that the eyes remain moist, the airflow has to be regulated. It was found that false eyelashes cause evaporation and increase the number of dust particles getting into the eyes.

*

Cold urticaria is an intense physical reaction to low temperatures. Symptoms may include skin rashes, hives, swelling, fatigue, anxiety, headaches, and breathing problems. Cold urticaria can be triggered by the weather, swimming in cold water, air conditioning, or by drinking cold beverages.

*

Trainsurfing has been practised since the 19th century. Following the American Civil War, it became a popular means of transport by those who were unable to afford to travel.

During the 1980s it became an extreme hobby amongst teenagers in South Africa. It has spread across countries – in Mumbai adrenaline junkies "surf" by hanging out of open carriage doors while performing stunts and tempting fate as they dodge steel pylons that run along the side of tracks.

The sport has become more popular with the use of social media where footage of the adventures is uploaded for all to watch. One group has taken things a step further by performing in their underwear.

*

The word *rhubarb* can mean a heated argument or dispute (although it is not often used nowadays in that context).

It can often be repeated by a group of actors/extras on a filming set to give the impression of indistinctive background conversation.

*

Arrector pili muscles are the tiny muscles between individual hair follicles. When the body is under some form of stress, nerve endings stimulate the arrector pili muscles to contract, which results in slight elevations of skin where each hair shaft emerges. These skin elevations are known as *goosebumps* because the person's skin looks like that of a plucked goose.

People who are open to the idea of listening to different types of music and allowing it to stimulate emotions are more likely to get goosebumps as a result.

*

Due to the effect that heat has on water molecules, a sponge will hold more cold water than hot water.

*

When "define anagram" is typed into Google's search engine, it will ask if you meant *Nerd fame again*.

*

Sir Hugh Beaver, the managing director of "Arthur Guinness, Son & Co (Dublin) Ltd", created a compendium of little-known facts to help settle obscure debates discussed in bars. The book, which was called the "Guinness Book of Records" was first released in 1955.

*

Guinness is not black nor dark brown – its actual colour is a deep dark red.

*

"Twinkle Twinkle Little Star", "Baa Baa Black Sheep" and "The Alphabet Song" all have the same melody. All are based on an 18th-century song which was written anonymously but made famous by Mozart.

*

In total, there were 365 episodes of the "Teletubbies" aired between 31st March 1997 and 16th February 2001. At one stage, it was the BBC's leading brand.

The show's creator was inspired by astronauts when he invented the characters. He thought that astronauts excitedly bouncing about on the moon wearing spacesuits made them look like they had oversized heads and shortened forearms, which was funny when compared to the achievement that they had just made.

*

The *pinky promise* originated in Japan and was known as "yubikiri" which translates as *finger cut-off*. In other words, if someone broke a promise or repeated a secret, they had to have their finger amputated.

*

On the 13th September 2001, Queen Elizabeth II broke protocol and allowed the troops to play the U.S. National Anthem during the "Changing of the Guard at Buckingham Palace" ceremony. This was the first time that this had happened and was as a tribute to the victims of 9/11.

*

British expatriate, John Green, bottled and sold Swiss air at a starting price of $97 for 500 ml; the cost for three litres was $247. Renowned for being healthy, the atmospheric commodity came with the instruction that it was best chilled in the freezer to enable the user to experience the full effect. The package also included a signed certificate of authenticity along with details of the GPS coordinates of the exact location it was taken from.

*

Sarah Breedlove (1867 to 1919) was born to former slaves and the first in her family to be born into freedom. Orphaned when 7 years old, married at the age of fourteen, she was widowed by the time she was twenty.

In the 1890s, Breedlove began to lose her hair, so she developed a tonic that she claimed made her hair grown back quicker than it had fallen out. With the help of her third husband, she started a successful advertising campaign which, when matched with her shrewd sales strategy, quickly led her to make lucrative profits.

The former washerwoman who earned $1.50 a day became America's first self-made female millionaire as well as being America's first black female millionaire.

*

Researchers from the Hebrew University of Jerusalem reckon that most people can guess the name of a stranger with up to 40% accuracy. The reason is that people grow to look more like their name by subconsciously changing their image and facial expressions. The research team also found that people could match a face to the name of a stranger correctly almost 50% of the time. The study concluded that faces can match names because of social norms and stereotypes as stereotypes become a "self-fulfilling prophecy".

*

Israel has the most advanced technology for drones and is the world's largest exporter of defence drones. They have sold drones and drone technology to more than two dozen countries.

A prototype of an unmanned aerial vehicle was allegedly used during an air raid conducted by Austria in 1849; they sent two-hundred balloons armed with time fuses and bombs to Venice. While some balloons successfully carried out the task, many were blown back into Austrian territory when the wind changed direction.

France and the Netherlands are training eagles to snatch illegal drones since small drones are often used to commit crimes or fly over restricted airspaces such as presidential palaces and military sites.

Drones have proven to be of great assistance to searchers and rescuers as they can get inside disaster zones and access hard-to-reach places without putting anyone in danger. They have been used in places like Haiti and the Philippines to map areas after a natural disaster - the drones were able to help teams establish which roads were accessible.

*

Pine cones are the reproductive parts of pine trees – the male pine cones are small and softish whereas the female pine cone starts out spongy, green and sticky, and grow into hard brown cones that protect seeds after they have been fertilised. Once the seeds have matured, the female cone opens up to let the wind distribute them.

In Shakespeare's time, pinecones were known as *pine apples,* - a name that was later transferred to the tropical pineapple shaped like a pinecone.

*

Buildering (which is also known as urban climbing) – is the inner-city version of rock climbing which has gained popularity in Russia. Using an assumed name of Max Polatov, one urban climber has been breaking into buildings in Moscow since he was 17-years-old. The height and adrenaline addict has been defying the security forces and risking arrest and possible imprisonment to follow his obsession. Scaling building and objects without any safety equipment, Polatov usually does some form of acrobatics near the edge at the top. The stunts are documented on camera at more than one-hundred metres above ground level. Regardless that numerous deaths have occurred the craze is on the increase.

Alain Robert (b 1962), the French "builderer", is probably the most famous. Known as the French Spiderman, he was 32-years-old when he climbed the Empire State Building. Over the years, Robert has scaled more than 120 buildings and been arrested more than 100 times. The most recent was in January 2019 when he climbed the G.T. International Tower, a 47-storey skyscraper in Makati City, Philippines. (The building is named after its owner, George Ty, and stands 712.93 feet tall (217.3 meters)).

Robert has fallen seven times during his career - the highest fall was from the height of forty-nine feet. He has been in comas and has fractured wrists, heels, arms, elbow, pelvis, and his nose.

*

During World War II the American government set the maximum speed at 35 mph in an attempt to conserve fuel and tyres. This gave the mechanical engineer and inventor, Ralph Teetor (1890 to 1982), the idea for cruise control. He was also responsible for creating other vehicle improvements, which included an automatic transmission. The interesting fact is that Teetor lost his sight after an accident when he was just 5-years-old. Afterwards, his sense of touch was heightened, which helped him to solve problems that other engineers found too difficult. He was so successful that he went on to become President of the Society of Automotive Engineers.

*

On the 30th June 1966, Irv Gordon (from New York) picked up his new Volvo P1800. With Gordon's passion for road trips, the car clocked over 3,000,000 miles. At that stage, it still had its original engine; in fact, the first thing that needed to be replaced was the clutch, but even that was only after 450,000 miles.

When he celebrated reaching one million miles, Volvo gave him a brand-new 780 Bertone Coupe. On its second millionth anniversary, Volvo gave him a new C70. Despite having new vehicles, Gordon preferred driving his trusty P1800, which got him recognised wherever he went.

*

Highway Hypnosis is what drivers experience when they are unable to recall part of their journey. It is most likely to occur when a driver is on a mundane or familiar journey and does not need to read the road signs - they are not entirely engaged in the task of driving but not necessarily being inattentive.

One theory is that the brain behaves in the same way as it does under meditation, i.e. it is in a relaxed state but should an incident occur the driver can react as quickly as usual. However, others debate that viewpoint – they believe that highway hypnosis does cause accidents. They argue that when a driver has "zoned out" they have slower reaction times, which may explain why some accident scenes do not have skid marks.

*

Didaskaleinophobia is the fear of school or the fear of going to school. It is most common in children between the ages of four to 6-years-old and is often because they are leaving the safety of their home for the first time. Another source may be the fear of bullies or travelling on the school bus with other children; it may even be that there is a fierce dog on the way to school that they have to pass.

Older children between the ages of thirteen to fifteen are also in a category that is most likely to suffer from didaskaleinophobia as it is around that age that they not only have to deal with more copious amounts of challenging work, but their bodies are also undergoing changes.

Environmental and cultural issues also play a factor such as other children bringing weapons into school, bullying, or having to attend a new school due to family or personal reasons.

*

Airports that have high altitudes have longer runways as the elevation makes it more challenging for planes to land and take off. The low pressure that exists at extreme heights reduces air resistance, making it harder for an aircraft to slow down. Not only must the runway strips be longer but planes must be equipped with special tyres to be able to handle high takeoffs and landing speeds.

The Daocheng Yading Airport in China is the highest-altitude airport in the world – it is located at an elevation of 4,411 metres; the runway measures 2.61 miles.

The Qamdo Bamda Airport in China has the second-highest altitude - it is located at an elevation of 4,334 metres. It also has the world's longest runway measuring 5,500 metres (3.418 miles).

An average runway is 1.14 miles long. Denver International Airport has the longest airstrip in America - it measures 3.03 miles.

*

Just like fingerprints, every person's tongue print is also unique.

*

The two small dimples that are at the bottom of some people's backs are known as *Venus Dimples* (named after the Roman Goddess of Beauty). They are formed by a short ligament stretching between the posterior superior iliac spine and the skin. They are believed to be a mark of beauty and are apparently indicators of good health. They also facilitate good circulation around the pelvis area. They are hereditary.

*

Most people enjoy listening to their favourite type of music. Once the sound is heard, the rhythm and wavelength are detected by the middle ear and cause the eardrums to vibrate. This mechanical force is turned into electrical energy by the brain and deciphered by the cerebral cortex (i.e. the thinking part of the brain). The sound then travels to the centre of the brain that controls emotions. The final stage of the journey is at the hypothalamus, which is the area that controls the heart rate, blood pressure, body temperature, and the nerves in the stomach and skin.

Research conducted in Britain and Italy concluded that music can do so much more than just lift a person's mood as the listener's heartbeat syncs with the tempo of the tune. Listening to upbeat music accelerates respiration and heartbeat whereas listening to slow, meditative music has a calming effect on the body which regulates the breathing pattern and slows down the heart rate. Further tests were carried out to establish how music affects the two kinds of emotions that are related to it, i.e. perceived emotions and felt emotions – the study explained that a person can feel the sorrow of sad music, but it does not necessarily make the listener depressed.

Personality traits can also be reflected in the listener's preferred genre and indicate whether the person has high or low self-esteem; whether they are creative, or whether they are hard-working or a bit on the lazy side.

Music also has an impact when exercising as upbeat music can drown out the messages from the brain that are trying to let the person know they are tired. If the tempo is matched to the actual exercise being done, it can be significantly beneficial to the success of the work-out.

*

Hearing music associated with our past often evokes a strong feeling. Dementia sufferers can also benefit from music as it can tap deep into emotional recalls. Medical research and experiments have taken place whereby music was used to help severely brain-injured patients recall memories.

In all of these cases, familiar music serves as a soundtrack for a mental movie that starts playing in our heads.

*

The longest non-medical word in the Oxford Dictionary is *Floccinaucinihilipilification*. It has Latin origin and refers to the act of describing something as having little or no value.

In the American dictionary (Merriam-Webster), floccinaucinihilipilification is not recognised at the longest word. In fact, neither is antidisestablishmentarianism. To be entered into the dictionary, a word must meet specific criteria:-

- It is required to be in widespread use,
- it must have continued usage, and
- it needs to be used meaningfully.

The longest word in Merriam-Webster's Dictionary is currently *electroencephalographically,* which refers to an apparatus for detecting and recording brain waves.

*

Arnold Schwarzenegger made his movie debut in the 1970s film "Hercules in New York". He used the stage name *Arnold Strong*. However, his accent was so thick that his lines were dubbed after production.

*

With more than three billion people flying through the air each year, it is inevitable that a few passengers may die during the flight. Protocols vary from airline to airline, but they all endeavour to deal respectively with the situation. If available, a body would most likely be placed in a row of empty seats, or in the first-class or business section where there would be more space. An alternative that some airlines have is to place the deceased passenger on the floor of the galley at the back of the plane. When it is a full flight, and there is no room to relocate the body, it would be covered up and strapped into the seat. Singapore Airlines (which is no longer in service) had a fleet of Airbus A340-500 aircraft were the first to include a "corpse cupboard" which was large enough to store an average-sized body.

One airline representative was interviewed and shared old methods used to deal with death on a plane. One option was to place a drink in front of the deceased along with a newspaper, put eye-shades on the person, and adjust the seat to make it appear that they were sleeping.

Pilots are not exempt from dying during a flight: -

- In 2009, a 61-year old pilot for Continental Airlines passed away on the journey from Brussels to Newark. A relief pilot was onboard who, along with the co-pilot, safely completed the flight.

- In September 2013, the captain of a United Airlines flight from Houston to Seattle suffered a heart attack mid-flight. The plane was diverted, but the captain died shortly after being taken to hospital.

- In October 2015, the captain of American Flight 550 died during the overnight flight from Phoenix to Boston. The plane was diverted after the First Officer declared a medical emergency.

*

There is a replica of Noah's Ark in Williamstown, Kentucky, which is about twenty miles from Cincinnati. The "Ark Encounter" features a full-sized Noah's ark which was built according to the Biblical measurements – 300 cubits by 50 cubits by 30 cubits, which translates as 510 feet long, 85 feet wide, and 51 feet high. The ark replica was the brainchild of

Creationist Ken Ham, who is the President of "Answers in Genesis"; the project cost approximately $100 million to build.

The events of the ark being built to save Noah and his family from a flood are not only found in the Book of Genesis but also recorded in texts of Judaism and Islam.

In Genesis chapter 6, verse 3, Noah was told by the Lord that there would be a flood in 120 years, which would have been the maximum amount of time to build the vessel. However, it is not recorded that Noah was instructed to start building immediately – the instruction came after Noah became a father, and his three sons were grown up and married. Some scholars have calculated that Noah only had a time range of 55 to 75 years to complete the ark.

*

Buzkashi is the national sport of Afghanistan. Played on horseback, the aim is to gain control of a carcass left in the centre of the playing area and drag it into the scoring area.

Buzkashi translates as *goat grabbing,* and it is usually the headless carcass of a goat that is used. Twenty-four hours before the game begins, the body is gutted and soaked in water, which helps to prevent it from being easily torn apart during the game. On occasions, sand is also packed inside the carcass to give it extra weight.

In the past, a carcass of a member from an enemy tribe may have been used.

The best players, known as chapandaz, have participated in extreme and intensive training, which can take many years. Their horses also undergo a rigorous five-year training programme.

The prizes that are on offer include money, elegant turbans, and clothes.

*

Before modern-day refrigeration, people in Russia and Finland put brown frogs in their milk to keep it fresh. Recent studies on the amphibians' skin showed that they contain antimicrobial compounds, such as those found in prescription antibiotics.

*

Highly populated countries, such as China, are faced with the challenge of getting people up and down some of the world's tallest buildings in as quick a time as possible. In 2016, the Shanghai Tower was awarded a Guinness record for installing the world's fastest elevator - it can travel at 20.5 metres per second (67 feet/second).

*

Most bamboos flower just once every 60 to 130 years. The length of the flowering interval remains a mystery to botanists - when it occurs, it is considered a phenomenon. It is believed that all populations of an individual species of bamboo flower at the same time because they all originated from a mother plant and therefore carry the same genetic makeup. When bamboo blossoms gregariously, it uses so much energy that it dies. This means that all the particular species will flower and die at the same time no matter whereabouts in the world they are located.

*

The National flag of the Philippines, popularly known as the *Three Stars and a Sun,* is a horizontal flag with equal bands of royal blue, scarlet red, and a white triangle at the hoist. (In the centre of the triangle is a yellow sun and at each vertex of the triangle is a small star).

Usually, the blue band is at the top, but if the Philippines are at war, the flag will be flown upside down with the red band at the top. Section 10 of the *Philippines Republic Act 8491* states that the rules and law covering the national flag also provides penalties, such as a fine and imprisonment of up to one year, for people disrespecting the flag. When President Benigno Simeon Aquino III met President Obama at the United Nations in 2010 the Pilipino flag was flying upside down – the U.S. government issued an official apology after the error was pointed out.

*

Campylobacter is a bacterium commonly found on kitchen sponges which can cause Guillain-Barre syndrome. People who contract GBS experience their nerves being attacked by their own immune system rather than the immune system attacking the germ.

Symptoms are represented by numbness, pins and needles, muscle weakness, pain, problems with balance and coordination, and can even lead to paralysis. Experts have ranked the kitchen sponge one of the dirtiest items in the home as it contains up to 200,000 times more germs than a toilet seat.

*

Restaurant menus are rarely, if ever, given a thorough cleaning. After being swabbed, it was discovered that on average, a menu carries 185,000 bacteria. Most are not harmful, but some can cause respiratory infections.

*

Introduced in 1966, the Toyota Corolla was the best-selling car worldwide by 1974. It has remained one of the most popular cars globally ever since, with estimated sales of over 38 million.

*

A *peen* is the end of a hammerhead opposite the face. It is usually curved or spherical.

*

In humans, the *glabella* is the skin between the eyebrows and above the nose.

*

eBay was launched on the 3rd September 1995 under the name AuctionWeb. It was founded by Pierre Omidyar, a French-born Iranian computer programmer. The site was owned by Echo Bay Technology Group which was Omidyar's consulting firm. Omidyar tried to change the name to "echobay.com", but the domain name had already been registered, so instead he shortened it to eBay and registered the site in September 1997.

The first item to be sold on eBay was a broken laser pointer which was purchased by a collector of broken laser pointers!

*

Brontology is the study of thunder.

*

Male coin spiders mate with females that are four times their size. Not only do they have to avoid being eaten by the said female after they copulate, but the males have an unusual ritual. During the process, the male breaks off part of his genitals, which effectively plugs the female. Studies have concluded that since several males can effectively fertilise the same batch of eggs, the "plug" serves as a blockage to other male's sperm. The coin spider bits of the remainder of his sperm sac afterwards as it is heavy and slows him down. Without the added weight, he is more agile and can act as a bodyguard to the female ensuring that any offspring belong to him.

*

There have been some conspiracy theories as to why the lids of some pens have a hole at the top of them. Some people tend to put the lid in their mouth when they are writing, but this has led to occasions when it has been swallowed. The hole ensures the airway is not totally blocked as it enables the person to be able to breathe until help arrives.

*

There is a lake in an oasis found in the middle of the Chinese desert. Yueyaquan (known as Crescent Lake) is located 3.7 miles (6 km) south of the city of Dunhuang. Measuring 218 meters long, the spring-water lake is positioned on what was formerly an important stop on the silk route. Today, the lake and pavilion are very popular with tourists who can travel to it by camel.

*

A new species of slug has evolved that is endemic to Mount Kaputar in New South Wales, Australia. The fluorescent rosy-pink slug lives in beds of red eucalyptus leaves which scientists suspect could potentially serve as camouflage. The mountain is designated as an endangered ecological area as it is also home to several other unique invertebrate species such as the Kaputar hairy snail and the Kaputar cannibal snail.

*

Virgin Boy Eggs are considered a delicacy in Dongyang, China. The eggs are soaked, boiled, and then cured in young boys' urine, which is supplied by schoolboy volunteers.

*

Balut is commonly sold as street food in the Philippines. The fertilised duck eggs are incubated for approximately two weeks before being boiled and eaten. The embryo is accredited for supplying extra protein. The Filipinos believe it to be an aphrodisiac and it is known colloquially as *the viagra of the Phillippines.*

*

Fried tarantulas are considered something of a delicacy in Cambodia. Although they are one of the most favoured street foods, they are not (oddly enough) that tasty. However, what they lack in flavour they make up for in crunch! Not only is the snack a free-range burst of protein, but many believe that it makes people look more attractive. Tourists are advised to break off a few legs and eat them first as jamming the entire snack in at once results in too many stiff legs poking about which makes the spider feel like it is wriggling to get out. The surprise finish comes when the abdomen is bitten into, and a mouthful of gooey nuttiness flows out.

*

Power Energy Toothpaste is the world's first caffeinated toothpaste. Invented by an American entrepreneur (Dan

Meropol), the toothpaste is designed to give an immediate boost in the morning.

It can take coffee up to an hour to fully absorb through the stomach, whereas the toothpaste begins working immediately while still cleaning teeth.

*

Earl Sigurd was the first Earl of Orkney, (an archipelago in the Northern Isles of Scotland), and was considered one of the greatest Earls of Orkney as he ruled wisely and became very powerful during the 9th century.

However, he did make an enemy called Máel Brigte (also known as Máel Brigte the Bucktoothed) who ruled the eastern and northern parts of Scotland. To settle their differences, (which most likely were due to a dispute over territory), Sigurd challenged his enemy to a battle, but instead of making it an equal 40-man-a-side combat Sigurd tricked Máel Brigte by putting two men on each horse. Máel Brigte fought hard, but he wound up beheaded. With plans to keep his opponents head as a trophy, Sigurd strapped it to his saddle and commenced the journey home. However, en route, one of Máel Brigte's prominent teeth scratched Sigurd's leg, which became inflamed and infected, resulting in Sigurd's death shortly afterwards.

*

Bergy Seltzer (also known as *ice sizzle*) is the crackling sound that is made when icebergs melt.

*

The Blood Falls, located in the Taylor Valley of Antarctica's remote McMurdo Dry Valleys, is a flow of red saltwater cascading from the Taylor Glacier which makes the area look like a massacre crime scene. The water has very high salinity and is rich in iron which, when mixed with the waterfall, gives it a bright red colour.

Sealed beneath the glacier is a small body of water which contains a community of microbes which beat all odds to survive in an environment where there is no light, oxygen, nor heat. Antarctica's Dry Valleys are one of the most inhospitable environments on earth, so scientists have been amazed and somewhat bewildered to discover seventeen different types of microbes.

The Blood Falls are the equivalent of a five-story high building.

*

The sulcus (also known as a groove) between the buttocks is medically known as the *intergluteal cleft.*

*

The shape of a Pringle is known as a *hyperbolic paraboloid.*

*

The two tiny holes drilled into the tips of some pens are to ensure that the air pressure is equal both inside and outside, which will make the ink flow smoothly.

*

The South Korean emergency number 113 is used to report a spy.

*

In recent reports, it has been disclosed that police in Mumbai have been using bananas to recover stolen goods! In 2016, a thief who had just snatched a gold chain from a woman decided to swallow it as he was being chased by the police and needed to conceal the evidence. After an x-ray was performed, doctors recommended surgery to retrieve the stolen item. However, as a more cost-effective method, the culprit was force-fed forty-eight bananas. Once the chain was recovered, the man was ordered to wash and disinfect it before handing it back.

In 2015, it was reported that another gold chain was recovered by making the thief eat two dozen bananas which were washed down with several litres of milk laced with laxatives.

*

Ancient Egyptians used reeds tied together in columns to hang on windows and doorways to create privacy in their homes. In ancient China, bamboo was used for the same purpose. The concept travelled through the Middle East and eventually into Europe. It gained popularity in Venice where it got the name of Venetian blinds.

The famous piece of artwork, the Venetian Blind, by Edmund Tarbell (1862 – 1938) is displayed at the Worcester Art Museum in Massachusetts. It is an image of a scantily clad woman showing her bare back with a Venetian blind giving her privacy from the outside world.

*

Angel Falls, the world's highest waterfall, is situated in the Canaima National Park in Venezuela. At the height of 979 metres (3,212 feet), it has the longest uninterrupted drop of 807 metres (2,648 feet). They are approximately fifteen times as high as the Niagara Falls.

The Angel Falls were unknown to the world until they were accidentally discovered by an American aviator, James Angel (1899-1956). His plane crashed at the site, and while all on board were unharmed, it took them eleven days to finally make their way out of the jungle.

During rainy seasons, the water often divides into two separate waterfalls. At this time, the water level is at its highest and subsequently at its strongest, which makes it possible for the spray to be felt as far away as one mile.

*

Traffic in Sweden, (initially horses and carts), incipiently used the right-hand side of the road until people suddenly started using the left-hand side in 1734. Historians speculate that this may have been because it was easier for right-handed people to wield their swords.

In 1916, the Swedish government made the switch back to having the traffic use the left-hand side, but it remained on the legislative agenda to be reviewed each year. A national referendum was held in 1955, and although the majority wanted to continue using the left-hand side, intense lobbying continued until the decision was made in 1963 to return to using the right-hand side. On the 3rd September 1967, the traffic stood still from 4:50 am until 5:00 am at which time drivers switched to the opposite side of the road.

The odd thing is that while drivers used the left-hand side of the road, they also drove left-hand vehicles, which would have made it very difficult to overtake another driver. The most accepted reason for this is that since most cars driven in Sweden at that time were American, it was not cost-effective to produce right-hand vehicles for such a small market.

Trains in Sweden generally keep to the left-hand side.

*

Except for Earth, every other planet in the solar system is named after Greco-Roman mythology (i.e. a Greek or Roman god). The word *earth* is derived from the Anglo-Saxon word *erda*, which means soil or ground, and the Germanic equivalent *erde*.

*

Due to gravitational forces, the earth is not perfectly round - technically it is a triaxial ellipsoid. There is a bulge around the equator, which means that anything at that point will be higher. Mount Chimborazo in Ecuador benefits from this fact as it makes it the highest point on earth – or the closest to space.

*

The original Christmas comedy-drama movie "Miracle on 34th Street" was released in the summer of 1947 as the studio production team believed that more people go to the cinema in warmer weather. The movie was rated as a "B" by the Catholic Legion of Decency which meant that it was morally objectionable in part because one of the main characters was portraying a divorcée.

*

Although not in common usage any more, the word *spermology* means the study of trivia. It comes from the Greek word *sperma*, which means *seeds*, and is, therefore, a study of seeds. A collection of small seeds or segments of trivia and general knowledge can metaphorically sprout into a tree of knowledge.

Humans have fourteen facial bones.

The definition of letters being described as uppercase or lowercase reflects the way that print shops were initially organised. Compositors stored the individual pieces of metal type in boxes known as cases. The large letters, i.e. the capitals, where stored in cases positioned on top of those containing smaller letters and the metal type for punctuation.

At approximately 840,000 square miles, Greenland is the largest island in the world. However, even though it is considered as an island, it is the twelfth largest country in the world.

There are many different beliefs in what makes a place either a continent or an island. Factors include tectonic independence, unique flora and fauna, cultural uniqueness, and how the inhabitants view themselves. Greenland is not geologically independent as it sits on the North American tectonic plate. Although it does have various unique species of plants, its animal life, such as arctic foxes, polar bears, and reindeer, can be found elsewhere. While it does have its own culture, it is considered part of the broader North American arctic culture.

The majority of Greenlanders consider themselves as islanders.

As well as being the lowest continent in the world, Australia is also the driest inhabited continent on earth. It is also the only continent without glaciers and without an active volcano (although there are two active volcanoes off the continent of Australia but within the Australian territory).

*

Penguins have to maintain a balance of salt in their bloodstream, which is challenging when their food and drink has such a high salt load.

Their kidneys are small and can only filter out enough salt to produce urine that is about one-third the concentration of seawater. The remaining excess salt is filtered out by the supraorbital gland which is located just above the eye socket – it is a type of lateral nasal gland which removes sodium chloride from their bloodstream.

*

The tradition of celebrating mothers is traced back to Greek mythology when spring festivals were held in honour of the maternal goddess, Rhea, who was believed to be the mother of many deities.

During the 1600s, Britain started to celebrate Mothering Sunday on the fourth Sunday of lent when, after a prayer service held in honour of the Virgin Mary, children presented their mothers with flowers.

In America, female activists, Julia Ward Howe (1819–1910), and Anna Jarvis (1864-1948) both campaigned for mothers to be celebrated. Their efforts were recognised on 8th May 1914 by President Wilson who signed a Joint Resolution designating the second Sunday in May as Mother's Day. However, Jarvis later disproved of the result as the holiday became commercialised, resulting in the original sentiment being sacrificed for profit.

One of the most unusual ways that Mother's Day is celebrated is in Yugoslavia. Children creep into their parents' bedroom and tie their mother up. The only way that she can be released is by presenting her children with gifts.

*

Babies born within nine to ten months of each other are known as *tandem twins*. In the U.K., the record for the smallest age gap between two siblings who are not twins is just 6.5 months; Ronnie and his sister Sienna were born only 208 days apart.

The longest gap between siblings is 41 years and 185 days. Elizabeth Ann Buttle gave birth to her first baby when she was 19 years old. Buttle, after conceiving naturally, gave birth to her second child when she was aged sixty.

*

Although records indicate that the first human cannonball made an appearance in New York City in 1873, there is a conflicting report claiming that the act was first performed in Sydney, Australia, in 1872. Regardless of which version is correct, the fact remains that one of the first and youngest human cannonballs was 14-year-old Rossa Matilda Richter.

Travelling at speeds up to 70 mph these human missiles can be shot to an altitude of 75 feet and a distance of 200 feet away.

While the mechanics of the equipment have not been fully disclosed it is understood that gun powder is only used to impress the audience by creating a loud bang and a puff of smoke to instil a more visual intrigue.

To project a person through the air, either compressed-air or bungee cords are used. Due to the extreme G-force, human cannonballs have been known to black-out in mid-air.

Landing is the most dangerous parts of the act; Richter broke her back when she missed the landing target, which led to her retirement.

*

Scientists reported in 2014 that when body weight is lost, it is actually exhaled via the lungs as carbon dioxide.

*

Participants from Greece always march first during the opening ceremony of the "Olympic Games," in recognition of the country's status as the first nation to ever hold both the modern and ancient version of the games. The Greek team is then followed by each country taking part in alphabetic order (by the local tongue); the host nation is always last in the parade.

*

When astronauts spend long periods in space, their hearts become more spherical and lose muscle mass due to the zero-gravitational force. Although astronauts' hearts return to their normal shape after they return to earth, scientists are not sure whether the physiological changes affect their health in the long-term.

*

On the 1st of April 2016, it was reported that people with tattoos were banned from entering Disney theme parks. While it turned out to be an April Fool's Day joke, Disney actually can refuse admittance if a visible tattoo is considered inappropriate, e.g. those containing offensive language or objectionable designs.

*

A cat's whiskers are so sensitively programmed that even the slightest move triggers a signal that is sent to the brain. The proprioceptors (sensory organs at the tips of the whiskers) are responsive to pressure, and if they are too close to an object, the cat can suffer from *whisker stress*. One of the most common causes of whisker stress is food and water being served in a bowl that is so small the whiskers touch the side of it. Owners may conclude that their cat is either picky about their food or not hungry, but the reality is that the cat would choose to go hungry than be subjected to whisker stress.

*

The "World Naked Bike Ride" is an event that was formed through collaborations with activist groups and individuals around the world in 2004.

Naked bike rides were not a new concept as they had taken place in several countries beforehand, but since the introduction of the WNBR popularity has steadily increased.

Although full (or partial) nudity is encouraged, it is not mandatory – the dress code is *bare as you dare*. While the majority of people use bicycles, some participate using skateboards or inline skates.

Not only do these peaceful events raise awareness of cyclists vulnerability and the dangers they face, but they also promote a healthy lifestyle.

*

The origin of the phrase "go commando" is uncertain. In Britain, it is speculated that it was used during the Second

World War as a euphemism for prostitutes working in London's West End who were referred to as the *Piccadilly commandos*. In the United States, it was thought to be associated with soldiers who fought in the Vietnam War who were reputed to go without underwear to increase ventilation which in turn reduced moisture and minimalised the risk of bacterial infection. The term gained popularity when it was used multiple times in the T.V. show "Friends".

*

Margery Meanwell was an orphan who was so poor she only possessed one shoe. After a wealthy gentleman presented her with a new pair of shoes, she excitedly put them on and ran about shouting *two shoes, see two shoes*. As a result, Meanwell was given the nickname *goody-two-shoes*.

Meanwell's story was a re-telling of the Cinderella story as she worked hard and eventually married a wealthy widower. The fable was written in 1766 by Oliver Goldsmith.

*

A landmark legal ruling was made in London, England, in September 2013 when two men were successfully prosecuted under the anti-litter legislation for spitting in the street. Their reparation was £300 each.

*

A humans' big toe is known as a *hallux*. In cases where the second toe is actually larger than the big toe, it is referred to as *Morton's Toe*.

*

The word *orange* has almost no perfect rhymes. The only word in the historical English 'Oxford Dictionary' and the American

'Merriam-Webster' that rhymes with orange is *sporange* (a rare alternative to the word *sporangium* - a botanical term for a fern or similar plant).

*

Mikey Finn was the keeper of Chicago's 'Lone Star Saloon' in the late 19th/early 20th century. He allegedly drugged his customers so that he could rob them. The meaning of the slang saying "to slip someone a mickey" is to lace their drink with a drug or incapacitating agent without their knowledge with the intent to take advantage of them.

*

TASER is an acronym for *Thomas A. Swift's Electric Rifle* which was the title of a young-adult adventure novel written by the author Victor Appleton (which was actually a pseudonym used by the Stratemeyer Syndicate which had numerous ghostwriters).

The first record of an improvised TASER being used was in the 1960s when American police officers used electric cattle prods to disperse Civil Rights activists. Although various inventors developed variations of the TASER, it was John Cover (1920 – 2009), a NASA researcher, who is accredited for the invention as (in 1974) he was the first to patent the design for a weapon that immobilised a suspected culprit. He took inspiration from reading a newspaper article about a man who survived being shocked by an electric fence and visualised the benefits an electric weapon would have when used as an alternative in situations where firing a gun should be avoided, e.g. during a mid-flight airplane hijacking.

*

Since his death in 1977, Elvis has remained one of the top

earning celebrities in the world. An income of $40 million (£32m) in 2018 ranked him in second place. Since 2013, the top-earning dead celebrity is Michael Jackson who has reportedly earned between $90 million (£72.9m) to $825 million (£668.7m) each year since his death in 2009.

*

At the age of 88 years old, Charlie Chaplin passed away on Christmas Day 1977 after suffering a stroke during his sleep. He was buried on the 27th December 1977 in a cemetery by his home near Corsier-sur-Vevey, Lake Geneva, Switzerland.

Almost four months later his family received a phone call to say that his body had been stolen and that they would have to pay $600,000 for its safe return; the grave robbers also threatened the lives of family members if their demand was not met. The police tapped the family's phone along with two-hundred other phones in the area. The approach was successful as two refugees from Eastern Europe were arrested, and the body was recovered (which was re-buried but this time the grave had a concrete covering).

The graverobbers appeared genuinely sorry for their actions and wrote letters of apology to the family. Regardless of their remorse they were still prosecuted for grave robbing and attempted extortion - one was sentenced to four years while the other received an eighteen-month suspended sentence.

*

Beavers' front teeth contain iron which makes them strong, sharp, and orange. Their incisors grow continuously and are maintained by their self-sharpening wear-down pattern.

*

Buckingham Palace has 775 rooms covering 828,821 square feet. It is estimated to be worth over £2.2 billion.

*

Mildred J. Hill (1859-1916) was an American songwriter who composed the melody for "Good Morning to All".

Her sister, Patty S. Hill (1868 – 1946), a composer and teacher, added the words "Happy Birthday to You" to the melody in 1893.

Both were posthumously inducted into the "Songwriters Hall of Fame" in 1996.

When the song became popular the third sister Jessica, fought to establish legal copyright for her sisters and it was officially published as "Happy Birthday" in 1935. The copyright was registered by the Summy Company who used several specific piano arrangements and an unused verse of the song. Over time, Warner/Chappell Music acquired the company holding the rights to the song and continued to insist that no one could sing the song publicly at a profit-making event without paying royalties. This was overturned in 2013 when a U.S. district judge ruled that the copyright originally filed by Summy Company was for a specific arrangement of the song and it, therefore, belonged to the public domain.

The last public performance that Marilyn Monroe did was on Saturday 19th May 1962 when she sang "Happy Birthday" to President John F. Kennedy.

The song had its longest distance broadcast in 1969 when the crew of Apollo 9 sang it to Christopher Kraft, the director of NASA.

*

Before the edible ice-cream cone came into existence, both paper and metal versions were used in England, France, and Germany, before the 19th century.

The first report of edible cones was recorded in the late 1800s by people who visited Germany. Although no one is totally sure who should be accredited for the invention, the first patent was granted in December 1903 to an Italian immigrant, Italo Marchiony. A similar creation was independently introduced in America at the 1904 St. Louis World's Fair by Ernest Hamwi, a Syrian waffle maker, who began rolling his pastries into horns to help out a nearby ice-cream vendor who had run out of dishes.

*

The collective noun for a group of geese on the ground is a *flock* or a *gaggle*.

A group of geese in flight is known as a *skein* unless they are flying in a "V" shape at which time the group is collectively referred to as a *wedge*.

*

Barn owls have lop-sides ears. Having one ear higher than the other helps them to detect where tiny sounds are actually coming from.

*

The events recorded as "The First Supper" capture the story about Frank McNamara who hurriedly changed his suit before going to a restaurant and subsequently forgot to take his wallet with him. The embarrassment led to the idea that the equivalent of a charge-card (which had become popular in American department stores during the late 1940s) should be created for restaurants. McNamara convinced many restaurants to sign up for the card which was launched in 1950; within one year the *Diners Club Card* had 42,000 members. The idea quickly gained popularity and became a status symbol amongst New York's business elite.

McNamara thought that the credit card would be just another fad and sold his shares for $200,000. However, popularity steadily increased, and by the mid-1960s the Diners Club had 1.3 million cardholders and was accepted worldwide. By 1957 McNamara had lost all his money and died following a heart attack.

*

Clowder is the collective noun for a group of cats.

*

If the 16-digit number on a credit card begins with a 4 it is a Visa card; if the number starts with a 5, it is a Mastercard.

*

Matt Groening is an American cartoonist, writer, and producer famous for being the creator of *The Simpsons*. His father was called Homer, his mother was called Margaret, and his younger sisters were named Lisa and Maggie – all names of the main characters in the TV Show.

Bart was given his name due to the fact it is an anagram of brat.

*

The triangular space located on the underside of a horse's hoof is known as a *frog*.

*

"The Adventures of Pinocchio" first appeared as a serial in an Italian magazine for children during 1881. Written by Carlo Collodi (1826 to 1890), the book was dark and cruel and ended with Pinocchio being hanged for his incalculable faults. Readers demanded that that was not the end so, along with two other characters, the blue fairy brought him back to life and turned him into a real boy.

Pinocchio was made from pine wood.

*

They are five species of prairie dogs which are all biologically related to chipmunks, groundhogs, marmots, squirrels, and woodchucks. Prairie dogs are rodents (a gnawing mammal distinguished by strong, continually growing incisors) native to North America; they live in tight-knit family groups called *coteries*. Although the females of the group remain together for life, the males tend to change coterie from time to time.

Prairie dogs are celebrated for their value to the ecological system: -

- They create intricate underground colonies (known as *prairie dog towns*) which act as shelters for jackrabbits, toads, and rattlesnakes.

- When they graze they create bare patches of ground which attracts insects which in turn become a food source for a variety of birds.

- Prairie dogs themselves are a food source for the endangered black-footed ferrets as well as other animals and birds such as badgers, coyotes, eagles, hawks, ravens, and snakes.

Over thirty years of research concluded that their vocabulary is much more advanced than any other animal language that has been decoded – some say that it is even more complex than that of dolphins and chimpanzees. Although their squeaky calls sound repetitive it has been discovered that they can convey extremely accurate details such as the direction a predator is coming from, the speed that it is travelling, and its size and colour. They even have a specific call that describes a human carrying a gun!

*

More people drown in freshwater than in salt water which is partially to do with the chemistry of water and how it relates to osmosis, i.e. the process that causes water to pass through the wall of a living cell.

With regards to ions, freshwater is more dilute in comparison to the fluid inside a person's lungs. When fresh water rushes into unprotected lung cells, it causes them to swell and burst. When capillaries in the lungs are exposed to freshwater, they become weakened and therefore are unable to stop the water from entering the bloodstream where it thins the blood down causing a disruption to the heart's electrical activity triggering ventricular fibrillation. The drowning person may have a cardiac arrest within as little as two to three minutes.

When saltwater is inhaled, the high salt concentration initially prevents the water from crossing into lung tissue. Drowning usually occurs because there is either no intake of oxygen or that carbon dioxide is not being expelled. When saltwater enters the lungs, the reaction of ions causes the blood to become thicker and to pull more blood into the lungs. As the blood thickens, a strain is put on the circulatory systems – this stress on the heart can lead to a cardiac arrest within eight to ten minutes.

*

The chemical formula for gold is *AU*, a derivative of the Latin word *aurum* which means *glowing dawn*. It is often suggested that *aurum* has a connection to the Roman goddess of the dawn – Aurora.

The weight of gold is measured in *carats* – one carat is equal to 200 milligrams. The purity of gold is quantified in *karats* with pure gold being 24 karats. If a gold coin is referred to as being 18-karats, it means that eighteen parts of pure gold were used with six parts of another metal being added to make the coin hard and durable. The other metal is usually silver, but it may be a mixture of cadmium, copper, iron, nickel, palladium, platinum, and zinc.

The hardness of a material or mineral is directly related to its atomic structure. Pure gold is so soft that a single gram can be beaten into a sheet of one meter^2. The reason for the softness is due to the atomic nuclei in gold being held together by a cloud of electrons which drift through the structure instead of having one set of electrons dedicated to one nucleus.

Gold that has been hammered into thin sheets is known as *gold leaf,* which is sometimes used to decorate food and drink – a practice that was initially regarded as medicinal. Gold leaf is flavourless and only used to promote a perception of luxury and high value. As pure gold is chemically inert, it passes through the digestive system without being absorbed into the body.

*

Israel's first President, Chaim Weizmann (in office 1949 – 1952), referred to Albert Einstein as the greatest Jew alive.

In 1952, Einstein received a letter from the Embassy of Israel enquiring whether he would accept the job of being president if it was offered to him. Einstein replied that while he was deeply moved by the offer he was also saddened and ashamed that it could not be accepted as, in his own opinion, he lacked both the natural aptitude and the experience to deal with people.

*

Cashmere wool is one of the most expensive and luxurious natural fabrics. It comes from cashmere goats which originated in India and Pakistan although in ancient times they were also found in China and other neighbouring countries such as Mongolia.

A cashmere goat can produce up to six ounces of under-down each year, which is then combed off when spring arrives. It takes between three to five goats to produce enough material to make an average-sized sweater.

One of the most famous factories which process and turn cashmere wool into garments is located in Elgin, Scotland. It was founded in 1797 and is the oldest factory still in production.

*

For many year rumours have circulated that people scatter the ashes of their cremated loved ones at Disneyland! The most popular rides where this occurs are the "Haunted House" and the "Pirates of the Caribbean".

It is claimed that the practice of scattering ashes has become so popular at the theme park that attendants have been briefed on how to handle such incidents and crews use specially equipped vacuums to collect the ashes.

*

On the 1st January 1913, the *Parcel Post Service* was launched in America. Specific guidelines were issued, which gave some parents the bright idea that it was actually possible to mail their children to relatives for their summer holidays. One famous case was that of 5-year-old Charlotte May Pierstorff (1908 to 1987) who was mailed to her grandmother's house seventy-three miles away. This was not the first incident but because the girl was so young it did push forward an inquiry into the matter and ultimately led to the decision that mailing children was forbidden. However, the practice continued for another two years until a 3-year-old, named Maud Smith, was posted to her grandparents, which highlighted the issue again and forced authorities to act accordingly. Fortunately, and unlike how many people imagined, children were not put into boxes fitted with air holes and loaded with cargo but instead they had stamps attached to their clothing and were accompanied by postal workers on their journey.

*

The King Cheetah (also known as Cooper's Cheetah) was first discovered in Zimbabwe in 1926 by Major A. Cooper; it has only been spotted in the wild about six times since then. The King Cheetah has stripes as well as spots which initially lead people to assume that they were a separate species. However, some have been born in captivity which enabled scientists to investigate the reason for their unique markings.

In 2012, it was discovered that the king cheetahs have a recessive mutation in their transmembrane aminopeptidase Q (Taqpep) gene which is responsible for causing the distinctive fur patterns.

They have been known to exist in Botswana, Zimbabwe, and

in the northern part of South Africa's Transvaal Province.

*

Cyprus has become renowned for its critical bird poaching problem with a reported figure of 1.7 million birds being illegally killed during 2016.

Throughout the migration season, the island is a favourite spot for birds to rest. However, many of these much-loved garden species, such as blackcaps, chiffchaffs, lesser whitethroats, and song thrushes, are lured to a cruel death by fake birdsongs being played from MP3 players which deceive the birds into believing that the area is safe. As they swoop down to land, they fly directly into a nearly-invisible net which can trap up to four-hundred birds at a time. At least sixty types of birds that are listed as threatened or in need of protection are snared in these illegal traps.

Laws forbidding such hunting techniques have been in place since 1974, but the practice has steadily increased by criminal gangs who sell their catch on the black market. The birds eventually end up in restaurants across the island where they are served in a traditional dish known as *ambelopoulia*. This controversial dish is served as a starter course - the diner has the choice of having the bird grilled, pickled, or boiled. Apparently, the birds are eaten whole.

*

Going to the bathroom in ancient Rome was not a private matter. While the marble-seated toilets may have appeared sophisticated, they were quite literally "public" - the user had the option to chat to their neighbour at the same time as conducting their personal business. The cleaning process involved the use of a *spongia,* which was basically a sponge kept soaked in a basin until the next person needed it.

*

In 1973, the American talk show host, Johnny Carson (1925 - 2015), cracked a joke on T.V. about a toilet roll shortage. This was on the back of real events occurring such as the stock market crash, and reports indicating that fuel, electricity, and onions were in short supply. Carson's joke caused people to rush out to the shops and stock-pile toilet rolls, which left supermarket shelves empty. Some shops tried to put a limit on the amount that one customer could purchase, but it was too late - for the next three weeks there actually was a shortage, and it took four months before the situation was under control.

*

For centuries pirates have been associated with the *Jolly Roger* – a flag illustrating a skull with crossbones symbolising terror on the high seas as it indicated that they had the intent to attack and steal.

An early record indicated that during the 17th century, the background colour of the flag was either red or green. The change to solid black possibly originated amongst the Barbary pirates (who were from North Africa) which would connect the flag to solid-black flags flown in Islamic tradition.

Bartholomew Roberts and Francis Spriggs allegedly used the same name for the flag as far back as 1721 and 1723 respectively. Other historians claim that the source of the name was a translation from the French *jolie rouge*, meaning *pretty red*, while others think that the flag was named after the first man who flew it – King Roger II of Sicily.

Historically, when a pirate ship was preparing to attack a

solid black flag would have been flown to indicate that as long as there was no resistance, no-one would die. A solid red flag would be used to say that no mercy would be shown.

Today the flag is used by various military and paramilitary organisations.

*

It is theorised that pirates wore an eye patch to keep one eye adjusted to darkness while up on the top deck. When they went below deck, they moved the patch to the other eye, which meant that they could instantly adapt to the extreme change in light.

*

The *Puente de Piedra* is a bridge that was built in 1610 in Lima, Peru. The interesting fact about the bridge is that the mortar was mixed with egg whites rather than water - today it is known as the *Bridge of Eggs*. However, this was not the first bridge to have eggs in the mortar; recently scientists scanned and tested the grout of the Charles Bridge (which crosses the Vltava River in Prague) which had been built during the 15th century and established that it contained egg proteins.

*

Scientists have discovered that the feeling we experience when tickled causes us to panic and evokes a response of uncontrollable laughter. While this isn't something new, and the debate still goes on about whether you can or can't tickle yourself on the roof of your mouth, more recent research found that schizophrenia impairs the predictive process that informs the brain that an act is voluntary. This can lead to lower recognition of voluntary actions and incorrectly attribute the cause to an external factor. A research experiment that was conducted found that people with high schizotypal scores (i.e. those prone to schizophrenia-like traits) did not find self-tickling to be any less ticklish than being tickled by someone else.

A study on rats showed that they liked being tickled. Under special audio-equipment, it was possible to hear their squeals rise; when the tickling stopped, they ran after the hand to make it tickle them again.

A medieval form of tickle-torture involved soaking the feet of a restrained victim in salt or sugar-water. A goat would then begin to lick the victim's feet which would initially have been ticklish. However, as the feet were constantly re-soaked the coarse tongue of the goat started to blister the skin, and it would eventually peel off, causing the victim to scream in pain.

*

Porn star, Lisa Sparks, born October 1976 in Kentucky, had 919 sexual partners in one day. The contest was held in 2004 in Warsaw, Poland, and to date, she still holds the title to the *Annual World Gangbang Championship*.

*

Following the death of her second husband in 2010, great-grandmother, Sheila Vogel-Coupe, started a new career as a prostitute. In 2016, at the age of 87, it was believed that not only was she the oldest person in the trade in the U.K. but most likely in the world. During an interview, she claimed that being lonely in her 80's was the reason for starting the new job. On average, she entertains ten clients each week and earns £250 per hour.

*

Donald Duck's address is 1313 Webfoot Walk, Duckburg, Calisota.

*

The surname *Duck* ranks as the 2,447th most common name in Great Britain. In the United States, it ranks as the 7,253rd most common surname with the census taken in 2000 showing that only 4,242 individuals had it as a surname. Some believe that it is of medieval Scottish origin.

*

The only country where you can watch the sun rising over the Pacific Ocean and setting on the Atlantic is Panama.

Panama is also the only country in the world that has a waterway that connects the Atlantic to the Pacific Ocean. All vessels going through the canal have to pay a toll which is based on the type of vessel, its size, and its cargo. An expansion was completed in June 2016 which enabled vessels to use it which were previously too large to do so. One of the first ships to avail of this had to pay a toll of $829,468.

The cheapest toll of 36 cents was paid by Richard Halliburton (1900 to 1939) when he swam the length of the canal.

*

Chinese whispers is the name given to the party game in which one person whispers a message to the person next to them, and the story is progressively passed to others until the last person announces what they heard - usually this only contains a small accurate portion of the original.

Until the mid-20th century the game was known as *Russian Scandal*. There are two theories as to why the name changed – firstly, many Western people find the Chinese language incomprehensible but do not mean it as offensive or racial (expressed in the same manner as to say something sounded double-dutch). However, others believe that the Chinese are thought of as being chaotic and unorganised and do imply a negative national stereotype.

*

To *drown the miller* means that too much water has been added to something, usually whisky, and therefore the good has been taken out of it.

The phrase dates back to the time when a miller was an important person within a village as he provided flour - without him, there wouldn't be any flour, and therefore no one would have any bread.

*

Bushu-suru is Japanese slang which literally means *to do the bush*.

When the phrase is used, it is in reference to an incident in 1992, when the American President, George H. W. Bush, became ill while attending a state dinner in Tokyo. After the second course, which was raw salmon with caviar, he fainted. As the president lay slumped on the table, he vomited onto the trousers of his host, Prime Minister Kiichi Miyazawa. When consciousness was regained, he told the physician to roll him under the table until the dinner event was over!

*

In 2010, a new species of snub-nosed monkey was discovered living in the forest of Northern Burma. The monkeys' characteristics differ from other snub-nosed species as they have black fur and prominent lips. However, the most distinct feature is their wide upturned nostrils which fill with water when it rains, causing them to sneeze. Known as the *sneezing monkey,* they can be found spending rainy days sitting with their heads tucked between their knees to avoid water going into their nose.

*

Camel urine can be as thick as syrup! The benefits of drinking it are mentioned in the Hadith (an account documenting the words, actions, and habits of the Islamic prophet, Muhammad) but the World Health Organisation has advised against it as it can lead to MERS (Middle East Respiratory Syndrome Coronavirus) which can cause fever, breathing problems, kidney failure, pneumonia, and even death.

In 2015, Saudi authorities closed down a shop in the city of Al Qunfudhah in south-western Saudi Arabia as the owner had been cost-cutting in the sales of traditional camel urine by filling the bottles with his own bodily waste.

In Egypt, a woman can be swapped for twenty camels; in Somali, the exchange rate can be as high as fifty camels for a woman and one-hundred for a man.

*

The first fatal car accident occurred in the U.K. on the 17th August 1896 when a car travelling at 4 mph struck a pedestrian called Bridget Driscoll (1851 – 1896). Witnesses said the car was moving as fast as a horse could gallop – like a fire engine. This occurred just a short time after an Act of Parliament had increased the speed limit up to 14 mph. The inquest lasted approximately six hours with the jury returning a verdict of accidental death.

*

Caligynephobia is the fear of beautiful women. Symptoms include general anxiety or nervousness, or even panic attacks.

The fear of men is caller *arrhenphobia*.

Scientists claim that they have proven that mice (and rats) are more afraid of men than they are of women. This is due to the chemicals that are produced naturally, and it is the smell that the mice are scared of. Mice just aren't anxious about human males – they are fearful of other male mice which produce a similar scent.

*

Qatar (officially known as the State of Qatar), which is located in Western Asia, is the only country name that begins with the letter "Q".

Iraq is the only country with the name ending with a "q".

*

The word *alphabet* originates from the first two letters of the Greek alphabet – *alpha* and *beta*.

Words were initially written from right-to-left, but then a new method was introduced whereby the direction of writing alternated with each line. It wasn't until the 5th century A.D. that the Greek settled into using the left-to-right pattern that we still use today.

*

William Ewart Gladstone (1809 to 1898) has been the only British Prime Minister to serve four times. He also served as the Chancellor of the Exchequer four times. When he resigned at the age of 84-years-old, he was Britain's oldest prime minister.

*

Glamorgan sausages are traditional Welsh vegetarian sausages which contain cheese, leeks, and breadcrumbs, as the main ingredients.

*

The *Blarney Stone* is found in Blarney – a small village located five miles northwest of Cork, Ireland. Legend has it that anyone who kisses the stone will receive the "gift of the gab", eloquence, or the skill of flattery. Each year more than 400,000 people visit the stone and follow tradition by lying down on their back, with their head hanging over a precipice, and stretch to reach the stone to kiss it. For this reason, it has been named as the most unhygienic tourist attraction in the world.

One myth suggests that it was the actual rock that Moses struck with his staff to produce water for the Israelites during the exodus from Egypt. However, an archaeologist has claimed that the original stone was moved sometime during the 19th century for health and safety reasons which suggests that the tourists are all kissing the wrong stone!

Today the name is used in various locations, such as Amsterdam, Australia, France, Germany, Pennsylvania, and Vancouver, as the name of an Irish pub.

*

The second most unhygienic tourist attraction in the world was *Gum Wall* in Bubblegum Alley located in Seattle at Pike Place Market. The tradition of sticking gum to the brick wall began in the 1990s by theatregoers who stuck their used tasteless gum there while waiting in line - some pieces were made into designs and colourful patterns. Declared as a tourist attraction in 1999 it attracted visitors until it was cleaned off in 2015. However, market officials do expect it to reappear over time.

*

Oscar Wilde died from meningitis on 30 November 1900. He was buried in a cemetery outside Paris, but nine years after his death his remains were disinterred and transferred to a graveyard inside Paris. His tomb became a tourist attraction, and it became a tradition to leave a lipstick heart on it. Hearts and words of condolences written in red lipstick or red spray-paint started to cause damage to the sculpture but cleaning it off caused even more stone to wear away. Wilde's tomb had to be protected by a barrier placed around it to keep loving vandals at bay but not before it was crowned as the world's third most unhygienic tourist attraction.

*

The advantage of thiols (also known as mercaptans - an organic substance made of carbon, hydrogen, and sulphur) is that they are an ideal additive to odourless gases as they make a gas leak easily detectable. Mercaptan is described as having the stench of rotting cabbages, smelly socks, or rotten eggs.

Skunks' spray consists mainly of three different thiols which produce an obnoxious chemical spray. Their scent glands can only hold about four ounces of liquid, and once it has been used, it can take ten days for the contents to be replaced. In light of that, skunks only use their spray as a last resort. If they are exposed to a dangerous situation, they will either run away or hiss and stamp their feet motioning that they are going to spray. This warning sign is often enough to make a predator retreat.

A skunk can control how they spray - it can either spray as a mist which will cover a wider area, or aim directly at the target in a direct stream which can travel up to sixteen feet. After the chemicals have been released, the smell can be detected up to one mile (1.6 km) away.

*

La Tomatina is an annual food-fight festival held on the last Wednesday of August in the Spanish town of Valencia. It was reported in 2012 that the festival had become so popular that around 50,000 people took part in throwing one hundred tons of over-ripe tomatoes at each other. Since then, official ticketing has limited the number of attendees to 20,000.

*

Black taxis in the U.K. have higher roofs than regular cars as they were initially designed to ensure they could comfortably accommodate a passenger wearing a bowler hat.

*

For the first time in thirty years, the "World Meteorological Organisation" published a new edition of its cloud atlas in March 2017 – it included eleven new types of clouds.

A *low-level cloud* is based below 6,500 feet; a *mid-level cloud* lies between 6,500 to 20,000 feet, while a *high-level cloud* is usually above 20,000 feet.

Cumulonimbus clouds can reach heights of up to 40,000 feet and are associated with thunderstorms and atmospheric instability. They can produce lightning and other severe weather conditions such as tornadoes.

No one is exactly sure where the expression to be *on cloud 9* comes from but the majority believe it refers to the cumulonimbus cloud which would mean that if you were on such a cloud, you are literally on top of the world. Some theorists suggest the number nine was chosen as it is considered a mystical number while others believe that the original saying was to be *on cloud 7* which was in connection to the Seventh Heaven mentioned in various religious teachings. The phrase is usually accepted in everyday vernacular to mean the best, happiest place to be, i.e. a state of euphoria.

*

From 1865 to 1958 the authorities in the town of Guanajuato, Mexico, required relatives to pay a grave tax – should they fail to do so their deceased loved ones were dug up and evicted from their grave. On 9th June 1865, the first body to be exhumed was that of Dr Remigio Leroy; it was discovered to be surprisingly well-preserved which was partially down to the extremely arid climate. The body was then stored in an ossuary in case the relatives decided on a reburial; by 1894 the ossuary had enough mummified bodies to open a museum.

As the bodies had been naturally mummified, they looked more horrifying in comparison to Egyptian mummies. Nearly all of the corpses' mouths are open as a result of the tongue hardening and the slackening of jaw muscles following death. Although they look like they are in terrible pain, most of them had died peacefully. However, three figures attract more attention: - a man who was stabbed with the puncture wound still visible; a man who drowned; and an unmarried pregnant woman who was buried alive by her own family with her hands covering her screaming face. The most recent addition to the collection was that of a six-month-old baby named Enrico who died in 1999 – although the parents could not afford the cemetery fees, they do visit the museum regularly to see him.

The "Guanajuato Mummy Museum" was voted as one of Mexico's best tourist attractions. The government have defended the museum stating that Mexico's culture is to celebrate the cycle of life and death. It is claimed that 99% of visitors say that they enjoyed the experience. Souvenirs can be purchased at the gift shop!

Mexican horror movies have used the mummies as props.

*

Lulu was a Vietnamese pot-bellied pig who lived in Beaver Falls, Pennsylvania. Her heroic act in 1998 brought her fame which included an appearance on both "The Oprah Winfrey Show" and "The Late Show with David Letterman".

When her owner, JoAnn Altsman, had a heart attack, the 150-lb pig squeezed through the dog-flap, pushed open the garden gate, and trotted onto the road where she lay down in the traffic. Eventually, one driver stopped and followed Lulu to where Altsman was lying. After open-heart surgery, the doctors told Altsman that had another fifteen-minutes passed she would have died. It was thanks to Lulu, who had suffered cuts to her stomach on her life-saving quest, that Altsman was still alive. Lulu was awarded the *Tiffany gold hero's medal* from the "American Society of the Prevention of Cruelty to Animals". She died at just five years old following a heart attack.

*

Dyngus Day is a Polish holiday held at the end of lent to celebrate Easter. On Easter Monday, it has become a tradition for boys to sprinkle girls with water or cologne and to whip them with pussy willow. The girls retaliate the following day by throwing dishes and cookware at the boys!

Historians believe that the custom commenced in 966 A.D. when Prince Mieszko I, and his court, were all baptised on Easter Monday. Today it is used as an opportunity for boys to flirt with the girl they like.

*

Situated in the Central Province, Sri Lanka, lies the capital city, Kandy, which is both an administrative and religious city. Kandy is home to the stunning 17th century "Temple of the Tooth" which is believed to house one of Buddha's left upper incisors.

It is told that the Buddha's tooth was removed as he lay on his funeral pyre. It was later smuggled to Sri Lanka in 313 A.D.

Today the incisor is kept in a two-storey shrine fronted by large elephant tusks. It is only removed once a year during the *Kandy Esala Perahera* (the festival of the tooth) which is a ten-day festival held to pay homage to it.

*

The call of the blue whale is claimed to be louder than a jet engine at take-off; it registers at 188 decibels. Believed by many to be the loudest animal on earth it actually ranks as the second loudest. The communication clicks of the sperm whale have been measured at 230 decibels.

*

The most commercially successful pop group, Abba, has only allowed two musical artists to incorporate part of their instrumental arrangement in their work - "The Fugees" used a sample from "The Name of the Game" on their 1996 single "Rumble in the Jungle", and Madonna's song "Hung Up" featured an instrumental introduction based on Abba's hit single "Gimme! Gimme! Gimme!"

In 1987, a British electronic band, The KLF, released a song called "The Queen and I" which sampled large portions of Abba's "Dancing Queen". However, Abba's songwriters, Benny Andersson and Björn Ulvaeus, had not given permission for this and it subsequently led to a legal battle. Although KLF travelled to Sweden intending to persuade Abba to let them keep the arrangement in the song, Abba refused to meet with them and demanded that the album was withdrawn from sale.

*

In 1991, 27-year-old Dr Helen Sharman was not only the first British astronaut but also the first female to visit the Mir Space Station as well as being one of the youngest people to go into space. Sharman, a qualified chemist who was working for the confectionary company "Mars Inc.", was one of almost 13,000 applicants who applied to the radio advertisement looking for interested applicants.

At 25-years-old, Gherman Titov (1935 – 2000), a Soviet cosmonaut, was the youngest person to go into space. He was also the first to vomit in space!

The oldest person to go to space was a 77-year-old American astronaut named John Glenn.

*

When viewed from space, the sun appears white. When sunlight is broken up using a prism, the colour range is red, orange, yellow, green, blue, indigo, and violet, which when mixed together appear white. The sun appears yellow to us because of the atmosphere; the closer it gets to Earth, the more the colours get altered, causing the sun to appear red.

*

A fly beats its wings approximately two hundred times a second.

*

Catgut is a cord made from the intestine of various animals – in particular sheep and horses (but not cats!). Once the membrane is chemically treated, the strands are woven into cords which are very strong and used for stringing musical instruments such as the cello, guitar, harp, viola, and the violin. Although the majority of musicians have switched to steel strings, many top players still rely on catgut as the industry has not created synthetics capable of reproducing the desirable qualities provided by gut strings.

In past times, catgut was used for medical suturing, but in more recent times it has been replaced with cotton and other non-animal products.

*

In 2014, the United Arab Emirates imported $456 million worth of sand, stone, and gravel. Despite being in the desert, Dubai was built with sand that was imported because desert sand is too smooth to be used in construction.

*

Ancient Greeks believed that the number 9 was a mystical number. Since cats are excellent masters at surviving falls, which is due to their balance reflexes and flexible backbones, they became an animal both to be worshipped and feared as it was commonly believed they were magical and had nine lives – three to play, three to stray, and three to stay.

*

The four suits in a pack of cards initially represented society: –

- *clubs* characterised both peasantry and achievement through hard work,

- *diamonds* illustrated the merchant class and success;

- *hearts* were a symbol for the clergy and the struggle to achieve inner joy,

- *spades* were symbolic for the warrior class institutionalised into the aristocracy.

Playing cards are deemed as one of the best examples of symmetry in design, i.e. the cards appear attractive as the human brain loves equilibrium, and secondly, the symmetry has a functional purpose as no matter what way the card is held it can be immediately placed into position without having to adjust its orientation.

*

America is the world's biggest producer of popcorn (followed closely by Canada and Australia); it is farmed in Illinois, Indiana, Iowa, Kentucky, and Nebraska. Although there are several varieties of maize, there is only one that will pop – the *Zea Mays Everta*. However, there are about one-hundred different strains of this corn, and each varies according to flavour, texture, and how they pop.

Kernels that don't pop are called *spinsters* or *old maids*.

*

The invention of the magnifying glass is accredited to the English philosopher, Roger Bacon (c1220 to c1292). The glass used is biconvex, which means that the lens bends the light twice, creating heat, thus making it easy to start a fire.

Farsighted glasses can also be used to start a fire because the type of glass used bends the light inwards towards a focal point (near-sighted glasses disperse the light instead of focusing it on one spot.)

*

Saudi Arabia imports camels from Australia for the primary purpose of being served in restaurants. As the Saudis focus on breeding animals for domestic and racing purposes, they do not have enough for their own consumption, particularly during the Muslim pilgrimage to Mecca (Hajj) when hundreds of thousands of camels are slaughtered.

*

Researchers in Tufts University, Massachusetts, successfully removed the eyes of young tadpoles and transplanted them into their tails. The study aimed to establish how their nervous system would adapt. Half the tadpoles were given the drug zolmitriptan (commonly used to treat migraines) - from that group, half-developed a network of nerves which spread from the eyes to their spinal cords. To establish how functional the eyes were, the tadpoles were trained to associate a red light with an electric shock. The tadpoles learned to avoid the red light, which was only possible if they were able to see.

The idea behind the experiment was to explore and understand how the nervous system can heal itself following an injury. The results showed the body could form working connections with transplanted organs, which in the future could assist researchers in finding ways to facilitate eye transplants and associated nerve growth.

Historically calories have been described as the amount of heat needed to raise the temperature of 1-kilogram of water from zero to 1°C.

Since 1925, physicists have described a calorie as the amount of work needed to force one newton through one metre (an energy unit known as a joule) which explains why calories are also referred to as kilojoules; one calorie is equal to 4.18 kilojoules.

Scientists measure calories by using a *bomb calorimeter* - a small chamber in which food is burned to heat water - the hotter the water gets, the higher the calorie count.

*

When Mayan ruins in Honduras were being excavated in 1931, a human jaw was discovered that had tooth-shaped shells implanted in it. This is one of the oldest pieces of evidence demonstrating that tooth-implants are not a modern-day invention.

It is believed that in ancient China, carved bamboo pegs were used to replace missing teeth while in Egypt, copper pegs may have been hammered into the jaw bone. A Celtic grave in France revealed a false tooth made from iron. However, experts believe that the Egyptians and the French may have inserted false teeth after a person died just to enhance the post-death smile.

Modern-day dental implants are made out of titanium. The idea was discovered accidentally in 1952 by an orthopaedic surgeon, Per-Ingvar Brånemark (1929-2014), who was unable to remove a titanium cylinder he had placed in a rabbit femur during a study of bone healing and regeneration. Following further research and experiments, the first titanium dental implant was successfully implanted to a human volunteer in 1965 in Sweden.

*

The word *mondegreen* is generally used to describe misheard song lyrics (although it can also be applied to speech). A well-known example is a line from Bob Dylan's song "Blowin' in the wind", which has the lyrics… "the answer my friend is blowin' in the wind" which is heard by some listeners as "dead ants are my friends, they're blowing in the wind".

Hearing is a two-step process involving sound waves travelling through the ear into the brain's auditory cortex. The next stage is the interpretation of the sound's meaning. Mondegreens occur when somewhere between the sound and the meaning communication breaks down, and the information is interpreted differently than it was intended.

Sylvia Wright, an American writer, published an article in 1954 entitled "The Death of Lady Mondegreen" where she discussed her own childhood mishearing. As her mother read to her a favourite Scottish ballad "The Bonnie Earl O'Moray" she misheard the two lines that went… "They have slain the Earl O'Moray, and laid him in the green", as… "they have slain the Earl O'Moray and Lady Mondegreen". After the article was published, the term mondegreen was adopted to describe any misheard song lyrics.

*

The band members of "ZZ Top" are Billy Gibbons (guitar) Dusty Hill (bass, keyboards), and Frank Beard (drums, percussion). Beard is the only band member who doesn't have a beard.

In 1984 Gillette offered $1 million to run an advertising campaign with their razor shaving the beards off – the band members declined the offer.

*

The *Pyrenean Ibex* (also known by the Spanish name *Bucardo*) was a subspecies of the Spanish ibex (wild goat) and is the only animal to have become extinct twice.

The last Pyrenean ibex was killed by a falling tree on 6th January 2000. Scientists took skin cells from the animal, and in 2009 an ibex was cloned making it the first species to become unextinct. However, the clone died several minutes later.

*

The Green-rumped parrotlet is one of the smallest species in the parrot family. With bright-green feathers and a little pink beak, it is considered the gentlest and most timid of the species. Researchers observed that parents teach their young a distinct series of sounds which they think are the equivalent of names. To test this theory, and to establish whether names were biologically programmed from birth or learned behaviour, a team of ornithologists swapped eggs between nests in a wild parrotlet population. The results showed that the chicks answered to the contact calls demonstrated by their adoptive parents; if the calls/names had been pre-programmed, the young would have used their biological parent's calls. Parrotlets are very social and having their own unique squawk/name helps them to identify one another.

*

In the late 1940s, scientists determined whether a female was pregnant or not by injecting a sample of her urine into a living frog. If the amphibian produced eggs within the following

24-hour period the result was positive.

Before this method was introduced, scientists used rabbits, mice, and rats, although they had to be killed a few days later so that an autopsy could be carried out. A positive pregnancy test would have a visible effect on the animals' ovaries.

*

David Holmes (born 1981), was the stunt double for Daniel Radcliffe in the Harry Potter movies, beginning with "Harry Potter and the Philosophers Stone" in 2001 until the filming of "Harry Potter and the Deathly Hallows" in 2009. His last stunt on the movie set went horribly wrong, and Holmes was paralysed from the chest down; it is reported that he now gets his adrenaline rush by driving specially-adapted cars around race tracks at speeds of up to 150 mph.

*

Daniel Radcliffe wore the same clothes every night for five months back in 2007. When he was starring in a play called "Equus", he noticed that if he left the theatre wearing the same outfit as the night before the paparazzi did not take any photographs as they would have looked like previous pictures and therefore could not be sold.

*

While countries usually celebrate Easter by observing Good Friday and Easter Monday, those living in Tasmania also get to celebrate Easter Tuesday. However, the public holiday is restricted mainly to those who work in government offices and education facilities.

*

Easter Saturday falls on the weekend after Easter Monday; it is not the Saturday between Good Friday and Easter Sunday.

*

Not all bees are yellow! The Blue Carpenter Bee is widely distributed throughout Southeast Asia, India, and Southern China and is distinguished by its hairy blue thorax, black abdomen, and large black eyes. These blue bees are essential pollinators and have proven useful by providing a service to farmers and fruit growers.

Blue Carpenter bees are generally not aggressive – the female is capable of stinging but seldom does so. While the males look very menacing, they do not have a stinger.

These bees do not lay as many eggs as other species. Often the female lays one batch of eggs and dies shortly afterwards as a result. The males die soon after mating.

The bees name is based on their ability to bore into wood to set up home.

Unlike honey bees, the Blue Carpenters do not live in a hive but instead prefer a solitary existence.

*

Pollen grains are the male minuscule particles released from trees, weeds, and grass. Their purpose is to fertilise other plants, but many remain suspended in the atmosphere, causing havoc in the lives of allergy sufferers.

A pollen count is measured by the thousands of grains per cubic meter. In Islamabad, the capital of Pakistan, the count can reach as high as 45,000 (although it did soar to 47,000 in March 2005). When Islamabad was founded in 1960, the authorities choose the *paper mulberry tree* as a signature tree because its ability to grow quickly would take away the barren look of the landscape within a short time. To achieve maximum propagation helicopters flew over Islamabad scattering paper mulberry seeds which quickly took hold.

Since then, the paper mulberry trees have been identified as the primary source of pollen.

To establish a pollen-count, the number of grains that land on a given area (such as a rod) during a specific time are stained before being examined through a microscope; fifty or less is considered a low count whereas 1,000 is considered very high.

The pollen season is divided into three main categories and timeframes: -

- tree pollen – from late March to the middle of May,
- grass pollen – from mid-May until July,
- weed pollen – from the end of June until September.

*

The study of insects is called *entomology*.

*

Fruit usually has a sticker attached to it known as a PLU code, i.e. price look-up number. There are three sets of numbers which indicate how the fruit has been grown: -

- if the PLU has four digits, then the fruit has been produced using conventional methods,
- a five-digit PLU beginning with the number 8 indicates that the product has been genetically modified,

- if the PLU has five-digits starting with the number 9 it suggests that the fruit has been organically grown.

*

During the Second World War, an incendiary device plummeted through the roof of a residential property. The occupants would all have been fatally injured had it not been for their dog, Juliana, who needed to go to the toilet at that precise moment; the device was diffused when the dog urinated on it! The Great Dane's actions earned her a Blue Cross Medal.

Three years later, in 1944, Juliana was awarded another Blue Cross Medal for warning customers in her owner's shoe shop that it was on fire.

*

The Kola Borehole is situated on the Kola Peninsula, Russia. The scientific drilling project commenced in May 1970 and lasted for twenty-four years. Measuring approximately 7 miles deep (almost 12 km), the borehole retains the world record for *depth-of-hole*; in comparison, it extends further than the bottom of the deepest ocean (the Mariana Trench in the Pacific Ocean is 6.8 miles underwater).

Drilling at such depths meant drilling at extremely high temperatures (180° C) which contributed to the project being stopped as the rock density was more like plastic rendering the drill-bits useless. Geologists were surprised when water was discovered deep within the earth where, in theory, it should not have been possible to be sustained. They also found 24 single-cell plankton microfossils.

Over time the borehole became known as the *Well to Hell*. It was reported that the temperature at the bottom was 2,000°C. It was also claimed that specially adapted recording equipment was lowered down the hole which recorded the screaming of tortured souls. One weekly tabloid informed its readers that the devil had emerged from the well and claimed the lives of thirteen rig workers.

Today the only evidence that the borehole exists is a rusty metal cap in the ground that has been welded shut.

*

Depending on the specific species, centipedes can have as little as fifteen pairs of legs or as many as 171 pairs. All types have an odd number of legs, so contrary to popular belief, they do not have one-hundred legs.

The legs of the first segment of the body are not used for walking but instead function as weapons that inject a paralysing venom into its prey – these appendages are known as *forcipules*.

*

The Manchineel Tree, found in Central America, South America, South Florida, and the Caribbean, is considered one of the most poisonous trees on the planet. Its fruit resembles a green crab-apple, but if eaten, can cause hours of agony – just one bite can potentially lead to death. The trees are so dangerous that even touching the bark can cause burns.

The trees' milky white sap is extremely caustic – one drop onto human skin causes blisters, dermatitis, swelling, or burns.

Burning the bark creates smoke that can cause temporary or permanent blindness. Even standing near a manchineel tree can cause death by asphyxiation.

On the plus side though they do provide ecosystem services such as acting as a natural windbreaker, and they protect beaches from erosion.

*

Although dogs have sweat glands on the pads of their paws, their primary method of cooling down is by panting, which causes the moisture on their tongue and the lining of their lungs to evaporate.

*

Ambidextrous people are equally skilled at using both hands.

On the opposite end of the scale are people who seem awkward using either hand – they are said to be *ambisinister*. Ambisinistrous motor skills are usually caused by handicaps and other debilitating physical conditions.

*

In parts of China, Korea, and Japan, it is common to see people wearing masks in public. However, contrary to popular belief, these masks are worn to protect other people from bacteria and not because the mask-wearer is afraid of contracting germs. They usually are worn when the person has a slight cold.

Over time they have also become a fashion accessory as they are faster to slip on when the wearer doesn't have time to apply make-up.

*

Beer manufactures in Japan stamp braille on the top of cans that spells out alcohol so that blind people can distinguish between a soft-drink and an alcoholic one.

*

There are various explanations as to why witches are depicted as flying on broomsticks.

Dating back to the Middle Ages, people have experimented with nature's provision of hallucinogenic products such as psychoactive mushrooms and poppy plants. Records from Medieval and Renaissance times have details of witch-based hallucinations following a potent hit of specific drugs.

One type of common drug used was processed rye-like plants, but consumption could be lethal. To get around the severe side-effects, smaller doses were administered by making it into an ointment and applying it to the mucous membranes (genitalia). The most common way to do this was on a narrow pole, and the most available pole in any house was that on a broomstick.

Another connection may have to do with pagan rituals. As a symbol, the broom was seen as a balance between masculine energies (the handle) and female energies (the bristles) which explains why it was used in marriage ceremonies.

The more innocent reason why broomsticks are associated with witches is that women always did the household chores, and as broomsticks were the tool of the trade every woman-owned one.

*

As a person falls asleep, the part of their brain responsible for reacting to various stimuli starts to relax – this includes the trigger-reaction that causes a person to sneeze.

The person's reflexes haven't been turned off, but rather the stimulation level has been raised so high that the amount of stimulation required to cause someone to sneeze would actually waken them up. This is the reason why people don't sneeze when they are asleep.

*

Honey is the only insect-created food that humans eat.

*

When Elizabeth Taylor died in 2011, she left specific instructions that her funeral service was to begin fifteen minutes after the announced start time. Renowned for always being late she also had someone at the service announce that she even wanted to be late for her own funeral.

*

In a study carried out in 1982, crayons were one of the top-ranking smells identified by participants. Their unique odour is basically beef fat, which is used to create the waxy consistency.

*

When someone has their eyes closed or has just rubbed them, they will usually notice little bursts of light and colours temporarily appearing across their vision. These strange light-bursts are known as *phosphenes* believed by scientists to be a light that comes from within the eyes.

Atoms continuously emit and absorb biologically produced light particles called *biophotons*, but the brain cannot distinguish between internal phosphenes and external biophotons, so the optic nerve simply relays light signals to the brain which makes the phosphenes visible.

*

Marvis Stone (1842 to 1899) is accredited with inventing the modern drinking straw; his product, made from paraffin wax-coated manila paper, was patented on the 3rd January 1888.

Straws are mainly non-recyclable and therefore, pose a

significant environmental threat.

The earliest known drinking straw was discovered in a tomb located in modern-day Iraq and was estimated to date back to between 2,000 B.C. to 3,000 B.C. – it was made from gold!

*

The length of a giraffe's tongue averages 20 inches. The males use their tongues to taste females' urine to establish if they are ovulating.

*

A *quidnunc* is someone eager to know the latest gossip.

*

In Greek mythology, Ambrosia was food that was brought to the gods by doves. It granted longevity or immortality to those that consumed it.

*

The flag of Nepal is the only national flag in the modern world that is not rectangular.

The flag of Switzerland and the flag of the Vatican City are the only square sovereign-state flags.

*

In 2006, a court in Maryland state ruled that *mooning* was a form of artistic expression and therefore protected by the First Amendment as a form of speech.

However, in 2013 in the U.K., a mother was jailed for one month after mooning at her son's school bus driver!

*

Cold weather can make the Eiffel Tower shrink by six inches.

*

Popeye is an uncle to a quadruplet of identical nephews named Pipeye, Peepeye, Pupeye, and Poopeye. They all dislike spinach.

*

In 1834, ketchup was sold as a cure for indigestion.

*

Jack Dorsey, the co-founder of Twitter, sent the first message on 21st March 2006 at 9:50 pm. It read "just setting up my twttr". In the early days, Twitter was referred to as *twttr* as it was a popular trend at that time to drop vowels in company names.

*

The average 8/9 minute shower uses about 65 litres of water.

*

Wolfsburg, which is the fifth-largest city in the German state of Lower Saxony, is famous for being the location of Volkswagen Group's headquarters, which is the world's largest car plant. Besides manufacturing cars, Volkswagen also produces pork sausages in Wolfsburg. In 2017, 6.8 million currywursts were made, which is higher than the number of cars that the factory built in that year. VW estimates that it produces about 18,000 sausages each day.

"As knowledge increases, wonder deepens."
Charles Morgan.

Time for a few random thoughts...

<u>Random thoughts</u>

Sweater is a weird name for a piece of clothing. Sweating while wearing a sweater makes you the sweater!

Where did all the ashtrays go when smoking bans were introduced?

There was a day when parents put you down and never picked you up again!

Earth is the most stressful place to live in the solar system.

People don't get stuck in traffic – they are traffic!

Why do we judge ourselves by our intentions yet judge others by their behaviour?

Why do people get offended by an accidental rump-roar yet say "bless you" after a sneeze which could potentially cause them to get a cold?

People will soon be able to trace their ancestors via Facebook!

Lemonade contains artificial flavours while furniture polish is made from real lemons.

Drinking alcohol is just borrowing happiness from tomorrow.

How can a fat chance and a slim chance mean the same thing?

A *ton of people* literally means 12 to 15 people.

Things are never on fire – fire is on things!

Is sand called *sand* because it is between the sea and the land!

Writing down reminders is a way to communicate with your future self!

Your stomach thinks all potatoes are mashed.